YOUR
DESTINY
IS CALLING

30 DIVINE MESSAGES OF
HOPE AND WISDOM TO HELP YOU GO
FROM SURVIVING TO THRIVING!

JONATHYN J. WILLIAMS

MILTON & HUGO L.L.C.
4407 Park Ave., Suite 5
Union City, NJ 07087, USA

Website: *www. miltonandhugo.com*
Hotline: *1- 888-778-0033*
Email: *info@miltonandhugo.com*

Ordering Information:
Quantity sales. Special discounts are granted to corporations, associations, and other organizations. For more information on these discounts, please reach out to the publisher using the contact information provided above.

Library of Congress Control Number: IN-PROCESS
ISBN-13:   979-8-89285-019-3   [Paperback Edition]
                  979-8-89285-020-9   [Digital Edition]

Rev. date: 01/15/2024

Acknowledgments

I am profoundly grateful to the individuals who have played pivotal roles in shaping both my personal and professional journey. Their immense support, guidance, and influence have left an indelible mark on my life.

To My Mom, LaShun Daniels: You have been my #1 supporter throughout my youth, showering me with unconditional love. Your teachings on keeping God first have been the cornerstone of my values. Your presence during times of adversity, your sacrificial efforts to meet my every need, and your unshakable discipline have sculpted my character. Raising three children as a single mother, you exhibited remarkable strength and character, and you were always there when I needed you the most. You kept me off the streets, kept clothes on my back, and always had a hot meal waiting for me.

To My Dad, Ernest Williams: Your active presence in my life has been a source of inspiration. You've shown me the true meaning of hard work and selflessness, always aspiring to provide a better life for me. Your sacrifices, putting my wants before your needs, and your accessibility have been invaluable pillars of support.

To My Brother, La'Qutin Peters: Thank you for consistently keeping it real with me, for paving the way for your younger siblings, and for being a true big brother and mentor. Your courage in building your own legacy has been an inspiration to me.

To My Sister, Shandaniecia Childress: Your love, akin to that of a son, has been a constant source of strength. Your willingness to show up when you didn't have to, being in position when I needed you most, and engaging in those late-night talks have been moments I cherish deeply.

To Roger and Idania Torres: Thank you for opening your arms to me, for imparting the essence of servitude, for taking a chance on me, and for the enriching conversations that have contributed significantly to my growth.

To My Spiritual Father, Rev. Dr. Michael Relton: Your love, akin to that of a father, has been a guiding light. Weekly Bible studies and your teachings on how to truly follow Christ have shaped my spiritual journey in profound ways.

To My Love, Betzaida Diaz: Your loving heart, openness to learn and grow closer to God's heart, and the trust you placed in me from day one has been a source of immense joy. Your patience during challenging times and your support, picking me up when I felt down, are treasures I hold dearly.

I extend my deepest gratitude to each of you for your immeasurable contributions towards me. Your influence has been musical notes for my instrument of life, and because of that I am truly grateful!

**With Love,
Jonathyn**

Table Of Contents

Introduction

Message 1: A Fight Worth Fighting

This message urges Christians to persevere in their faith, emphasizing the importance of fighting the spiritual battle described in 1 Timothy 6:12. It encourages believers to resist worldly temptations, stay true to God's Word, and find strength in the eternal life offered through Jesus, portraying the Christian journey as a challenging yet worthwhile fight for faith.

Message 2: A Shifted Mentality

This message emphasizes the significance of one's outlook in shaping their life's outcomes and advocates for stepping out of one's comfort zone to gain new perspectives. Drawing on biblical wisdom from the book of Proverbs, the author underscores the power of thoughts in shaping one's reality and encourages a positive mindset for personal growth and breakthroughs.

Message 3: Are You Ready

This message emphasizes the responsibility that comes with knowledge, blessings, and resources, drawing from Luke 12:48. It explores the transition from Moses to Joshua, highlighting Joshua's readiness for leadership, and encourages readers to reflect on their preparedness for life's challenges and tasks, emphasizing the importance of obedience to God's commands.

Message 4: Are You Updated

This message draws an analogy between spiritual growth and the continuous updates of technology. It emphasizes the importance of seeking God's daily guidance and staying spiritually updated to face current challenges, encouraging readers to embrace divine nourishment and wisdom for the present rather than relying on past experiences.

Message 5: Check Your Roots

This message emphasizes the correlation between faith and actions using James 2:26, highlighting the idea that faith without corresponding works is incomplete. It encourages readers to assess their actions as the fruit of their faith, stressing the importance of genuine commitment and effort to complement one's beliefs and achieve spiritual growth.

Message 6: Come And Follow Me

This message demonstrates various aspects of a Christian's life, including belief, repentance, prayer, studying the Bible, obeying commandments, worship, fellowship, and sharing the Gospel. It encourages believers to strengthen their roots on Earth by living in accordance with these principles and reminds them that their experience in heaven is influenced by how they live on Earth.

Message 7: Divine Disruption

This message highlights life's disruptive situations and encourages a perspective that sees these disruptions as indications of God doing something new. Drawing from Isaiah 43:19, the message emphasizes the need to focus on the future and embrace divine disruptions as a part of God's process for growth and positive change in one's life.

Message 8: Don't Give Up

This message draws from the book of Galatians, emphasizing the Apostle Paul's encouragement not to grow weary in doing good. It assures believers that, despite challenges and delays, continuing in good deeds will ultimately yield a harvest at the appropriate time, underscoring the importance of perseverance and trust in God's faithfulness.

Message 9: Finish Strong

This message emphasizes the biblical call to persevere and remain faithful despite life's challenges. Drawing inspiration from passages like Hebrews 12:1 and Matthew 24:13, the author encourages believers to complete tasks, honor commitments, and set positive examples, highlighting the importance of finishing well in aligning with God's purposes and inspiring others.

Message 10: Grow Where You're Planted

This message explores the Gospel of St. Luke, emphasizing the importance of faithful stewardship over small aspects of life, as illustrated by Jesus' teachings in Luke 16:10. The author encourages believers to focus on the present, be faithful in small matters, and trust that growth and abundance will follow in due time.

Message 11: I Believe

In this message the speaker explores the profound significance of belief in Christianity, drawing inspiration from Jesus' words in Mark 9:23. Emphasizing the transformative power of unwavering faith, the message encourages believers to anchor themselves in the unshakeable reality of God's kindness and grace, using the example of the woman with the issue of blood to illustrate the potency of belief in God's miraculous intervention.

Message 12: I Have A Plan

In this message the author delves into Jeremiah 29:11, emphasizing that God's plan for believers involves prospering them and providing hope and a future. Acknowledging the context of Jeremiah's prophetic message to those in exile, the speaker encourages patience and trust in

God's timing, emphasizing that even during challenging times, God has a purpose and a promise for a brighter future.

Messager 13: It's Time To Go

In this message the author explores the lesson of faith through the biblical account of Abram (later Abraham) in Genesis 12. Emphasizing the importance of leaving the familiar and stepping out in obedience to God's call, the speaker highlights Abram's transformation and willingness to embrace a new destiny, encouraging readers to reflect on their own faith, obedience, and acknowledgment of when it might be time to embark on a journey of divine purpose.

Message 14: It's Time To Serve

This message emphasizes the essence of leadership as servitude, drawing inspiration from the example of Jesus Christ. The author underscores the joy and fulfillment derived from selfless service, using biblical references such as the Parable of the Good Samaritan and Jesus washing His disciples' feet to illustrate the transformative power of humble acts of kindness and compassion.

Message 15: Joy Is Enough

This message emphasizes the distinction between happiness and joy, highlighting that while happiness is fleeting and dependent on external circumstances, true joy comes from a deep connection with the Lord. The author encourages choosing joy daily, emphasizing that it is sustainable, sufficient, and not reliant on material possessions but rather on a relationship with the Creator.

Messager 16: Keep The Vision

This message emphasizes the importance of maintaining focus on one's vision even when faced with obstacles, delays, or uncertainties. Drawing inspiration from the biblical figure Habakkuk, the author encourages perseverance, faith, and trust in God's timing, reinforcing the idea that the fulfillment of the vision may be delayed but will surely come to fruition.

Message 17: Living In Expectation

This message emphasizes the importance of expecting positive outcomes in faith. Drawing inspiration from biblical examples, the author encourages the audience to live each day with hope and a positive outlook, highlighting that expectation is a key determinant of faith. The message emphasizes the need to actively position oneself to receive the blessings one anticipates, reinforcing the idea that expectation is crucial for faith to be effective.

Message 18: Look In Your Hand

This message recounts a story of a man robbing a bank to get more money, only to later discover that the gun he used was worth double the stolen amount. Drawing a parallel to our desires and God's provisions, the author encourages the audience to recognize that God has already equipped them with everything they need for life and challenges them to discover the potential within their current possessions, emphasizing the value of resourcefulness and gratitude.

Message 19: Love Guided Actions

This message delves into the teachings of the apostle Paul in 1 Timothy, emphasizing the importance of instructing others with love. Using the example of Paul instructing Timothy to address false doctrines, the author underscores the idea that corrective actions should stem from a place of love, mirroring the grace and mercy received from the Lord.

Message 20: Perfect Timing

This message explores the concept of balancing anticipation of Christ's return with active ministry in the world, drawing inspiration from the Book of Acts. Emphasizing the importance of diligent work while patiently awaiting Christ's return, the author encourages believers to engage in meaningful actions and ministry, emphasizing the perfect timing of God's plan.

Messager 21: Purposeful Pain

This message emphasizes the inevitability of pain in life and draws inspiration from Romans 8:28, highlighting that all things, even hardships, work together for the good of those who love God. Using a baking analogy, the author illustrates that just as seemingly ordinary ingredients come together to create a delicious cake, challenges and pain in life are part of a transformative process leading to a higher purpose designed by God.

Message 22: Return To Me

This message recounts a personal experience of drifting away from God due to a focus on material wealth, leading to a sense of emptiness and challenges. Drawing from the book of Zechariah, the author emphasizes the need for sincere repentance and returning to God, highlighting that God is always ready to embrace and forgive those who genuinely seek Him.

Messager 23: Righteous Suffering

This message reflects on the biblical story of Job, highlighting his unwavering faith despite facing severe trials, including personal loss and suffering. The author draws parallels to personal challenges, emphasizing the importance of remaining steadfast in faith, relying on the protection provided through a close relationship with Jesus Christ, and recognizing the potential for spiritual victory over Satan's schemes.

Message 24: Step Into Your Destiny

This message encourages listeners to overcome past hurts and hindrances, emphasizing the need to let go of negative experiences that may block future opportunities. Drawing inspiration from Isaiah 43:18-19, the author urges individuals to move beyond past pain, embrace a new perspective, and trust in God's promises for a brighter future.

Message 25: The Gift Of Grace

This message explores the concept of grace as an undeserved gift from God, emphasizing that it is freely given out of His love and compassion. Using the analogy of earned trophies versus received presents, the author highlights that grace is not something to be worked for or earned but is bestowed upon individuals as a reflection of God's limitless love, encouraging a humble and open-hearted approach to receiving and sharing this transformative gift.

Message 26: The Who Behind The Why

This message reflects on the impact of catastrophes in life, using the example of the COVID-19 pandemic in 2020. The author suggests that sometimes God allows crises to occur to reveal Himself in new ways, emphasizing that God is present even in the midst of catastrophes and that these challenging moments can lead to a deeper connection with Him when people cry out for help.

Message 27: Unsinkable Faith

This message explores the story of Noah and the Flood, highlighting Noah's obedient and faithful response to God's command to build an ark despite ridicule and the lack of visible signs of a flood. The author draws parallels to contemporary scenarios, emphasizing the importance of faith, patience, and obedience in the face of God's directives, ultimately linking Noah's journey to the Christian call for unwavering faith and leadership within families.

Message 28: Waiting On God

This message reflects on Moses' transition to Joshua as a leader and emphasizes the importance of patience during seasons of feeling stuck or waiting for God's timing. Drawing from Deuteronomy 31:6, the author encourages listeners not to misinterpret temporary setbacks or unmet expectations as indications that God is finished with them, emphasizing the need to wait on God's timing and purpose.

Message 29: Who Are You

This message explores the search for true identity beyond worldly achievements, emphasizing the importance of understanding oneself in the context of God's purpose. Drawing from biblical figures like Moses, Paul, John the Baptist, and Mary Magdalene, the author encourages listeners to seek God's wisdom, recognize their identity as children of God, and find purpose through a transformative understanding of their unique calling.

Messager 30: You Are Called

This message emphasizes that one's calling transcends qualifications and worldly standards. Drawing from the biblical story of David, the author highlights that being called by God is more significant than meeting external expectations, and individuals should embrace their calling, trusting that God qualifies those whom He calls.

Introduction

Embark on a transformative odyssey with "Your Destiny is Calling," a compelling invitation to immerse yourself in a profound and life-altering adventure. Allow me to guide you through a tapestry of 30 powerful messages, each acting as a guiding light, directing you towards a life intricately shaped by destiny through God's word and your identity in Christ. This literary journey transcends the boundaries of a conventional book; it serves as a rallying cry, a call to action that resonates with the profound declaration that your celestial destiny eagerly awaits, and the opportune moment to seize it is now!

Prepare to transverse the realms of spiritual discovery, bask in the soothing waves of healing, and unlock the doors to your true purpose. This isn't merely a narrative; it's a roadmap for a purposeful existence, an opportunity to align your path with the greater power that awaits you. The pages of this book are not just ink on paper; they are a conduit for a deeper connection, a catalyst for transformation, and an embodiment of the divine whispers of your creator calling you towards your destined purpose.

As you delve into the captivating chapters, anticipate an expedition of self-discovery that transcends the ordinary. You are not just a passive reader; you are an active participant in the unfolding narrative of your own destiny.

The clock is ticking, and the cosmos is aligning in your favor. So, heed the call, embrace the journey, and let the transformative power of these 30 divine messages propel you into a future where your destiny unfolds in all its glory. The time for action is now, and the adventure awaits. I hope you're ready, because "Your Destiny Is Calling"!

A Fight Worth Fighting

The Bible states in 1 Timothy 6 that we are to "fight the good fight of faith." Verse 12 reads: "Fight the good fight of faith; take hold of the eternal life to which you were called, and for which you made the good confession in the presence of many witnesses." This means that even when it seems like we're losing, we must maintain our composure and keep going; therefore, we can refrain from giving up. If we hold fast to God's Word and do not give up, He will cause us to triumph.

Now, you might lose a round or two in the fight of faith, but just because you lose a few rounds doesn't necessarily indicate that you've lost the fight!

With that being said, this message is entitled "A Fight Worth Fighting."

Being a Christian places you in a position where you are constantly at war with your flesh, the ignorance and false teachings in this world, corrupted political standards, misconceptions, exploitations of ideologies, and Satan himself—all of which are opposed to the Lord and those who confess Him in faith.

By professing Jesus Christ as your Lord and Savior, you entered the Christian faith and declared yourself to be an enemy of the dark dominion. Your flesh is then allied with the ways of the world. Believe it or not, things of such are working day in and day out to force you to give in to what your human nature truly desires.

Now, it is not a battle with God but a joining of forces with Him against our common enemy. It is a spiritual struggle in which we contend with the world, the body, the devil, and our own self-will while remaining steadfast in the truth of God's Word.

Fighting the good fight of faith is more about overcoming obstacles in the Christian life or firmly grasping eternal life through Jesus than it is about engaging in combat against a physical enemy. When we fight the fight of faith, we are fully trusting in the Lord and growing in grace while developing a precious intimacy with Him as we abide securely in His love.

As the apostle Paul writes his letter to Timothy from the confinement of prison walls, he tells him (1 Timothy 6:3-4): "If anyone teaches false doctrine and does not agree with the sound teaching of our Lord Jesus Christ and with the teaching that promotes godliness, he is conceited and understands nothing." He later adds (1 Timothy 6:9-10): "But those who want to be rich fall into temptation, a trap, and many foolish and harmful desires, which plunge people into ruin and destruction. For the love of money is a root of all kinds of evil, and by craving it, some have wandered away from the faith and pierced themselves with many griefs."

But as the body of Christ, we must ensure that we separate ourselves from all these things and only be in hot pursuit of godliness, our faith, and most importantly, love. So, we must grasp the eternal life to which we were called and pursue the path of righteousness. Just as St. John said in 1 John 4:4, "But greater is He who is in you than he who is in the world."

Friends, I want to encourage you to exercise your heavenly artillery and fight the good fight. Every day is a battle. Every day is an opportunity. Every day brings opposition. Every day Satan is ready to use and abuse you and take away what's rightfully yours, and he wants you to surrender at the forefront of evil.

But in fighting the fight of faith, the Lord has provided everything needed to be more than a conqueror! Yes, it's a battle! Yes, it's a war! Yes, it's a brawl! Yes, it's tough! Yes, it gets difficult and tempting to give in at times! Yes, the world tries to show us other ways and temporary pleasures! And yes, it's a fight, but it's a fight worth fighting!

Prayer:

Heavenly Father,

As we come before you in prayer, we acknowledge the call to "fight the good fight of faith" as stated in 1 Timothy 6:12. Lord, help us to grasp the eternal life to which we are called and to hold firmly to the confession of our faith, even in the face of challenges.

We recognize that being a follower of Christ places us in constant spiritual warfare. In this fight against the forces of darkness, our own fleshly desires, worldly influences, and the schemes of the enemy, we seek Your strength and guidance.

Grant us the resilience to withstand the battles that come our way. Though we may encounter setbacks and losses, let us not lose heart but remain steadfast in our commitment to You. Help us to remember that even in moments of defeat, the ultimate victory is secured through our faith in Jesus Christ.

Lord, we understand that this fight is not against flesh and blood but against spiritual forces. Equip us with the full armor of God, as mentioned in Ephesians 6, so that we may stand firm in truth, righteousness, peace, faith, salvation, and the Word of God. In Jesus name we pray, Amen!

The key points of this message entitled "A Fight Worth Fighting" are as follows:

- **Scriptural Foundation**: The message begins with a reference to 1 Timothy 6:12, which encourages believers to "fight the good fight of faith" and take hold of eternal life.
- **Perseverance in Faith**: It emphasizes the importance of maintaining one's faith even when facing challenges, setbacks, or opposition. Believers are encouraged not to give up on their faith journey.
- **Spiritual Warfare**: The message highlights that being a Christian means being in a constant spiritual battle. Believers

are depicted as being at war with their own flesh, false teachings, worldly ideologies, and spiritual forces opposed to God.

- **Alliance with God**: It clarifies that the fight of faith is not a battle against God but a partnership with Him against common enemies. It's a spiritual struggle where believers contend with the world, their own desires, the devil, and self-will while staying grounded in God's Word.
- **Overcoming Obstacles**: Fighting the good fight of faith involves overcoming obstacles in the Christian life and firmly grasping the promise of eternal life through Jesus. It's about trusting in the Lord and growing in grace while abiding securely in His love.
- **False Teachings and Materialism**: The messages references Paul's warnings in 1 Timothy about false teachings and the love of money leading people away from the faith. It encourages believers to pursue godliness and stay away from harmful desires.
- **Greater is He Who is in You**: It cites 1 John 4:4 to remind readers that God's power within them is greater than any opposition or temptation in the world.
- **Exercising Spiritual Weapons**: The message encourages believers to use their spiritual tools and weapons to fight the good fight of faith, recognizing that it's a daily battle with challenges, temptations, and opposition.
- **A Fight Worth Fighting**: Despite the difficulties and temptations faced in the Christian journey, it is a fight worth fighting. Believers are encouraged to persevere, trust in God, and follow the path of righteousness.
- **Prayer**: The message concludes with a prayer, asking God to help readers learn how to fight the good fight of faith and find inspiration in the example of Jesus Christ.

Overall, this message underscores the idea that the Christian life is a continuous battle of faith, but it's a battle worth fighting, with the assurance that God's power within believers is greater than any opposition they may encounter. It encourages perseverance, trust, and a pursuit of godliness.

A Shifted Mentality

You will only think to the capacity to which you are exposed. We must understand that the importance of our outlook will determine our outcome.

A lot of times, we tend to stick with the familiar and want nothing to do with "the unknown." We would rather spend every single day following a routine that consists of the same people, foods, clothes, conversations, and activities.

Little do we know that when we do this, we put walls around our mentalities that block us from experiencing the fullness of the world and sabotage the pursuit of our destiny.

This message is entitled "A Shifted Mentality."

Do you really want to find out who you are? Do you really want to walk into what God has pre-destined for your life? Wouldn't you like to see what you're really capable of? The first step to all these things is simply getting out of your comfort zone and trying something new! Life is all about perspective. You will always see something the same way if you're looking at it from one perspective.

Would you believe me if I told you that the only difference between you and the people you admire is the perspective that they have on life? Here's a quote by American Artist Mary Engelbreit: "If you don't like something, change it. If you can't change it, change the way you think about it."

Here's another quote by the minister, William Constantine: "Your reality is as you perceive it to be, So, it is true, that by altering our perception, we can alter our reality."

The last quote I'd like to share with you is by someone unknown: "The proper perspective makes the impossible possible."

Friends, the substratum which I'm fully trying to articulate to you all goes back to my initial statement, which was, "You will only think to the capacity from which you are exposed to." Now that you have a general explanation of what we are shooting for, let's work on the Spiritual side of this! Let's go to the text, shall we?

I want to take a look at the book of Proverbs. If you're having trouble locating Proverbs in your Bible, it is the 19th book right after the book of Psalms. Let's take a glance at Chapter 23, Verse 7. It reads this way, "As a man thinks in his heart so is he." Before we discuss the fruit of this scripture, let me give you a little background on the book of Proverbs. The book of Proverbs was written by Solomon, the son of David, King of Israel. In previous books throughout the Old Testament, Solomon is considered the wisest man known to the ancient world. This book demonstrates practical skills for living well and thriving in the Kingdom of God!

The purpose of this book is to impart wisdom to its readers. But this wisdom is not merely a collection of facts and information; it is practical knowledge rooted in awe of the Lord. It is knowledge that God has established guidelines for the world, and if we follow them—His way, the path of wisdom—we will be blessed and prosperous. But if we reject the guidelines, we will make foolish decisions and do harm to both us and other people.

Now back to Chapter 23, Verse 7. "As a man thinks in his heart, so is he." Friends, your reality is a reflection of your mentality. It's eagerly important that you know what you think matters because it is birthing the foundation of who you shall become.

Recently, I picked up this book entitled "Strength-based Leadership" by Tom Rath. One of the things he discussed in his book that I noted was to start writing all your strengths on a sheet of paper. He went on to say don't just stop there but start saying those things to yourself daily. The moment that I started acknowledging that "I'm a great speaker," "I'm a great writer," "I'm a great leader," etc., I started to see it in the real world!

I want to encourage you and let you know that your breakthrough is on the other side of what you think in your mind. If you tell yourself you can't lose weight, then you won't. If you tell yourself you'll never find love, then you won't. But! If you shift those negative thoughts and change them into a more positive way of thinking, then you will start to see God open doors in your life that you never knew existed.

The last unexplored territory of our privacy that we possess is our minds, and in this journey called life, it's so easy for negativity to sneak into our brains. This means it is essential that we plant and water the seed of positivity, eagerness, and confidence in our minds so we can change the trajectory of our lives.

Prayer:

Heavenly Father,

we bow before you, grateful for the wisdom shared in the message of "A Shifted Mentality." Help us, O Lord, to grasp the profound truth that our thoughts shape our capacity, and our outlook determines our outcome. Forgive us for the times we've clung to the familiar, building walls around our mentalities, hindering the pursuit of the destiny You have planned for us.

As we reflect on the importance of perspective, guide us to step out of our comfort zones and embrace the unknown. Grant us the courage to discover our true selves and walk into the pre-destined path You have laid before us. May our minds be transformed by Your Spirit, aligning our thoughts with Your truth. Empower us to shift negative thinking into positive declarations, trusting in Your plan for our lives. Plant seeds of positivity, eagerness, and confidence in the unexplored territory of our minds, leading us on a trajectory of transformation. In Jesus name we pray, Amen!

The key points of this message entitled "A Shifted Mentality" are as follows:

1. **The Importance of Outlook:** The message begins by emphasizing the significance of one's outlook or mentality, suggesting that it plays a crucial role in determining the outcome of one's life.
2. **Comfort Zone vs. Exploration:** It points out that people often stick to their comfort zones, following the same routines and avoiding anything new or unfamiliar. This, it claims, can limit personal growth and sabotage one's pursuit of destiny.
3. **The Role of Perspective:** The message asserts that life is all about perspective and that one's perspective on life can make a significant difference. It suggests that the difference between individuals and those they admire lies in their perspectives.
4. **Quotes on Perspective:** It shares quotes from various sources that highlight the importance of changing one's perspective when faced with challenges or circumstances that cannot be changed.
5. **Biblical Reference:** The message refers to the book of Proverbs, specifically Proverbs 23:7, which states, "As a man thinks in his heart so is he." It connects this verse to the idea that one's reality is a reflection of their mentality.
6. **The Power of Positive Thinking:** The message encourages readers to recognize the power of their thoughts and to shift from negative thinking to positive thinking. It mentions the importance of affirming one's strengths and capabilities to bring about positive change.
7. **Breakthrough and Positivity:** It suggests that one's breakthrough in life is often on the other side of their thoughts. Negative thoughts can hinder progress, while a positive shift in thinking can open doors and lead to unexpected opportunities.

8. **Mind as Unexplored Territory:** The message emphasizes that the mind is an unexplored territory and that it's important to plant and nurture seeds of positivity, eagerness, and confidence in one's thoughts to change the trajectory of their life.

9. **Prayer:** The message concludes with a prayer, thanking God for the message and asking for a shifted and sharp mentality for the readers.

Overall, this message encourages readers to recognize the power of their thoughts, the importance of perspective, and the need to shift from negativity to positivity to experience personal growth and achieve their destiny. It suggests that a changed mentality can lead to a changed reality.

Are You Ready

The Bible says in Luke 12:48, "For everyone who has been given much, much will be required; and from the one who has been entrusted with much, even more will be expected."

I've learned that there is a great responsibility that comes with having knowledge, blessings, and resources. Join me as I embark on grasping the essence of the passing of Moses and the induction of Joshua.

This message is entitled "Are You Ready."

Before Moses died, his purpose was primarily focused on leading the Israelites out of Egypt and guiding them through the wilderness towards the promised land. He acted as the mediator between God and the Israelites, receiving the divine laws and commandments on Mount Sinai and teaching them to the people.

Moses served as a judge, settling disputes among the Israelites, and he played a vital role in establishing the religious and ethical foundation of the nation. Throughout his life, Moses demonstrated unwavering faith and obedience to God, working tirelessly to fulfill God's will and deliver the Israelites to the land flowing with milk and honey.

Though he did not enter the promised land himself, Moses ensured that the people were prepared and ready to inherit it, appointing Joshua as his successor to lead them forward.

In Joshua 1:1-9, the Lord spoke to Joshua, Moses' successor, commanding him to arise and lead the Israelites into the promised land. God promised to be with Joshua just as He was with Moses, giving him strength and courage.

Joshua was urged to meditate on God's Law day and night, obeying it faithfully. The Lord assured Joshua that no one would be able to stand against him if he followed God's commands. Joshua was encouraged to be strong and courageous, not to be afraid or discouraged, for the Lord his God would be with him wherever he went.

Now remember, Joshua was chosen by Moses and recognized by the Israelites as a man of courage and integrity. He was known for his obedience to God's commands and his unwavering commitment to follow Him.

Before Moses passed, he publicly appointed Joshua as his successor in front of the entire congregation, ensuring that the people acknowledged him as their new leader. This formal passing of authority provided a smooth transition for Joshua to step into his new role as the leader of the Israelites.

You see, friends, Joshua was determined to take the place of Moses. He recognized the weight of the responsibility and the importance of continuing the work that Moses had started. He witnessed the great leadership and guidance of Moses during their time together, and he understood the significance of leading the Israelites into the promised land.

His determination was evident in his faithfulness and loyalty to Moses as his assistant. He diligently learned from him, observed his relationship with God, and witnessed the miracles that God performed through him. This prepared Joshua to step into the leadership role with confidence and trust in God.

Since he was entrusted with so much, he knew the great expectations that came with it. It's safe to say that Joshua was ready for his new assignment.

Friends, are you prepared for the tasks and challenges that lie ahead in your life? Are you physically, mentally, emotionally, and spiritually ready to be inducted into the next task? Just as Joshua was appointed to lead the Israelites into the promised land, we too are called to fulfill our purpose and navigate the journey of faith.

Every day, ask yourselves these questions, and don't forget to check in on those around you. Ask them, are you prepared? Are you acknowledging the call? Are you obeying God's commands? Are you preparing for the battles and embracing your faith? Are you ready?

As we reflect on Joshua's readiness to lead the Israelites, let us examine our own lives. May we be inspired by Joshua's example as we actively prepare ourselves for the journey ahead. Remember, God equips those He calls. Be ready, dear brothers and sisters, and trust in His provision.

Prayer:

Heavenly Father,

We come before You with hearts open and willing to embrace the message of "Are You Ready." Your Word in Luke 12:48 reminds us of the great responsibility that comes with the blessings, knowledge, and resources You entrust to us.

Lord, as we reflect on the passing of Moses and the induction of Joshua, we recognize the importance of being ready for the tasks and challenges that lie ahead. Moses faithfully led the Israelites, and Joshua, in turn, embraced the responsibility of leading Your people into the promised land.

Just as Joshua was appointed and recognized, we seek Your guidance in acknowledging our callings and responsibilities. Grant us the wisdom to be physically, mentally, emotionally, and spiritually prepared for the tasks ahead. May we be obedient to Your commands and embrace the journey of faith with courage and strength.

Lord, help us to examine our lives daily, asking ourselves if we are ready for the assignments You have for us. May our hearts be open to Your leading, and may we actively prepare ourselves for the battles we may face, trusting in Your provision.

We pray for one another, that we may encourage and support those around us in their readiness for the tasks You have placed before them. May we, like Joshua, be determined to fulfill our purposes with faithfulness and loyalty, always leaning on Your guidance. In Jesus name we pray, Amen!

The key points of this message entitled "Are You Ready," are as follows:

1. **Scripture Reference**: The message begins with a quote from Luke 12:48, emphasizing the idea that with great blessings and knowledge comes great responsibility and expectation.
2. **Moses' Legacy**: The author discusses the role of Moses in the Bible, highlighting his leadership in leading the Israelites out of Egypt and guiding them through the wilderness. Moses served as a mediator between God and the people, and he played a pivotal role in establishing the religious and ethical foundation of the nation.
3. **Passing of Authority to Joshua**: Moses, before his death, appointed Joshua as his successor. Joshua was chosen for his courage, integrity, obedience to God's commands, and commitment to following God.
4. **Joshua's Preparedness**: Joshua recognized the weight of the responsibility and the importance of continuing Moses's work. He diligently learned from Moses and witnessed God's miracles through him, which prepared him to step into his leadership role with confidence and trust in God.
5. **Application to Our Lives**: The message urges readers to reflect on their own preparedness for the tasks and challenges that lie ahead in life. It encourages self-examination, obedience to God's commands, and readiness for the journey of faith.

6. **Prayer**: The message ends with a prayer, where the author asks for strength, courage, and faith to answer God's call for the next task and to trust in His promises.

Overall, The purpose of this message is to inspire readers to be prepared, faithful, and obedient in their own journeys of faith, drawing inspiration from Joshua's readiness to lead the Israelites. It encourages individuals to recognize the responsibilities that come with their blessings and knowledge and to trust in God's provision.

Are You Updated

This message is entitled "Are You Updated".

Battles of today cannot be fought with yesterday's bread!

Let's take bread from a package, for instance.

Consider a typical loaf of Wonder bread. Whether you purchase it in Texas, Washington, Louisiana, or any place in between, it will appear the same way. Wonder bread has a consistent appearance. It is mass-produced for a market of millions for maximum efficiency, always sliced the same way, packaged the same way, and scented the same way.

However, handmade bread is unique. Sometimes it rises unevenly, it's a little saltier, and other times the crust is thicker than the day before. That's because this particular bread wasn't produced by a machine. It is individualized. Hands are used to handle, knead, and bake it. Because of this, what comes out of the oven is not an exact replica of what came out of the oven the day before. It's still bread, though, so that's not to say. The attributes and components are the same. But the result will always be different from yesterday's.

The bread God provides for His children has a somewhat different appearance daily. Today's bread is neither the same as yesterday's bread, nor will it be the same as tomorrow's bread. While it always emerges from the heavenly oven with the same fundamental qualities of nourishment, sustenance, compassion, and grace, it takes on a somewhat different shape each time.

Jesus informs us in Matthew 6:11 to ask God for today's bread, not yesterday's bread or tomorrow's bread. But to pray "Give us today our daily bread."

You know, I did a study the other day on iPhones and iPads to see how many times a year they fix errors. I learned that often, Apple releases big software updates to help keep the iPhone fresh. They discovered that upgrading to the latest version of software provides the latest features, security updates, and bug fixes. Researchers went on to prove that it's important that you update right away because it fixes a security flaw that is already being used in real-life attacks. Studies have found that if you do not update when prompted, you'll start coming across a lot of bugs and performance issues, find your apps slowing, and you won't receive security updates on your iPhone, which could, of course, leave you at risk.

So, my question for you is…

Are you spiritually updated? Are you consistently internally upgrading to the latest version of divine software?

Are you fighting with today's bread, or do you have on yesterday's armor, trying to fight today's battles?

Friends, it is eagerly important that we (just like the iPhone) constantly update! The rest of this year bears a lot of fruit, but it also comes with a lot of satanic ambushes.

So, I challenge you to take the time to update so you can prosper properly.

Prayer:

Heavenly Father,

As we gather in prayer, we reflect on the powerful message titled "Are You Updated." We acknowledge, Lord, that battles of today cannot be fought with yesterday's bread. We thank You for the analogy of bread, illustrating the uniqueness and freshness of the sustenance You provide for Your children each day.

We recognize, Lord Jesus, your instruction in Matthew 6:11 to seek today's bread, understanding that it holds the qualities of nourishment, sustenance, compassion, and grace, tailored for the challenges we face now. Just as iPhones and iPads need regular updates for optimal performance, we too need to be spiritually updated. Help us to internalize the latest version of Your divine software, embracing the features of faith, love, and resilience. Grant us the wisdom to discern the spiritual updates needed to navigate the challenges and satanic ambushes of the days ahead. I Jesus name we pray, Amen!

The key points of this message entitled "Are You Updated?" are as follows:

1. **Analogy of Bread**: The message begins by drawing an analogy between mass-produced bread and handmade bread. Mass-produced bread is consistent and uniform, while handmade bread can vary in texture and flavor because it is individualized.
2. **God's Daily Provision**: The message highlights how the bread that God provides for His children is not the same every day. While it always provides the fundamental qualities of nourishment, sustenance, compassion, and grace, it takes on a slightly different form each day.
3. **Matthew 6:11**: The messages references Matthew 6:11, where Jesus teaches us to pray for "today's bread" and not yesterday's or tomorrow's bread, emphasizing the importance of seeking God's daily provision.
4. **Technology Update Analogy**: The author draws a parallel between updating software on devices like iPhones and iPads and the need for spiritual updates. They explain how regular updates provide new features, security fixes, and bug corrections.
5. **Importance of Spiritual Updates**: The messages challenges readers to consider if they are spiritually updated and whether

they are equipped to face the challenges of today. It stresses the importance of staying current in one's spiritual walk.

6. **Call to Action**: The author urges readers to take the time to update spiritually so that they can face the challenges and prosper in the current year. They encourage readers to seek wisdom and understanding to keep their faith up to date.

7. **Closing Prayer**: The message concludes with a prayer, asking God to grant wisdom and understanding to those who may feel it's too late to update spiritually. It also asks for confidence and a hunger to face life's battles with today's spiritual resources.

Overall, this message emphasizes the need for spiritual growth and staying updated with God's guidance to face the challenges of each day. It encourages readers to seek God's daily provision and to update their spiritual walk regularly.

Check Your Roots

James 2:26 "As the body without the spirit is dead, so faith without works is dead."

This message is entitled "Check Your Roots."

Your faith is your root, and your works (actions) are your fruit. You see, the way you determine a tree is by its fruit. If you see a tree with apples on it, then it is an apple tree. If you see a tree with figs on it, then it is a fig tree. Before it was an apple tree or a fig tree, it was first a seed planted inside the soil to form the roots that gave it the ultimate power to grow outwardly, what was placed within. It's safe to say that the tree is a replica of its roots!

Remember only faith can save us, and this saving faith will lead to good works. In the book of James, James argues that it's not individuals who don't do any good works that aren't saved, but simply because their lack of good works shows that they don't have any saving faith. In verse 16 of chapter 2, James articulates, "If one of you says to them, 'Go in peace; keep warm and well fed,' but does nothing about their physical needs, what good is it? (17) In the same way, faith by itself, if it is not accompanied by action, is dead." What James is saying coexists with what the Apostle Paul wrote in Galatians Chapter 6, verse 9. (Galatians 6:9) "Let us not become weary in doing good, for at the proper time we will reap a harvest if we do not give up." Paul claims that whatever you sow into your life is what you will get from it.

You can live a life that pleases God and live in purpose, on purpose. Or you can choose to live in sin and find yourself going in circles trying to fight a spiritual battle using worldly artillery. Abraham is one who was considered righteous for what he did when he offered his son Isaac on the altar. His faith and his actions were working together, and his faith was made complete by what he did. The scripture was then fulfilled when it says, "Abraham believed God, and it was credited to him as righteousness," and he was called God's friend.

This shows that a person is only fully considered righteous not just by faith alone, but by what they do to enact their faith. A couple of weeks ago, I had a great conversation with a man at my local grocery store. He shared with me how he used to be very overweight to the point where he could barely walk. As he continued telling his story, he said that day in and day out he would pray to the Lord about losing all this weight. The man then shared that even though he was believing and hoping for it, he still wasn't eating right, didn't work out right, and drank alcohol to subsidize the pain. He then told me that he had been doing that for 13 years and nothing ever changed. It wasn't until he started eating healthier, going to the gym more often, and letting go of the alcohol when he noticed that he was drastically losing weight.

The man concluded his story by telling me this quote, and that is "a job is only considered a job if all you do is clock in; it isn't until you get your hands dirty that then consider it work". Friends, the essence of what I want you to take from this is exactly what this message is entitled: "Check Your Roots." As I said earlier, your faith is your root and your works (actions) are your fruit! Sometimes we can exercise the mindset of "I have faith," but we have learned that faith alone is only 50%. What weight are you putting down on your faith that enables your root to spring forth fruit? Always remember that faith that is accompanied by action makes the impossible possible.

Prayer:

Heavenly Father,

We come before You with hearts open to the profound message of "Check Your Roots" based on James 2:26. We recognize, Lord, that just as a tree is known by its fruit, our faith is the root that determines the fruit of our actions.

As we meditate on the truth that only faith can save us and that saving faith leads to good works, we seek Your guidance in aligning our roots with Your truth. Help us, Lord, to understand that a genuine, living faith is one that bears fruit through actions and deeds.

We are reminded of the powerful illustration of Abraham, whose faith and actions worked together, making his faith complete. Grant us the wisdom to cultivate a faith that is not stagnant but active, producing fruits that glorify Your name. Lord, help us to check our roots daily, ensuring that our faith is vibrant, and our actions align with Your will. May we understand that true work is not just clocking in but getting our hands dirty in the service of Your kingdom. In Jesus. name we pray, Amen!

The key points of this message entitled "Check Your Roots" are as follows:

1. **The Analogy of Trees and Roots**: The message begins by drawing an analogy between faith and trees. It explains that just as you can identify a tree by its fruit, you can evaluate your faith by your actions. Faith is compared to the roots and works (actions) are likened to the fruit.
2. **Faith and Works Go Hand in Hand:** The central message is that faith and works are interconnected. True faith leads to good works, and it is through these works that faith is made evident. The absence of good works can indicate a lack of saving faith.
3. **James and Galatians Correlation:** The message highlights a correlation between James' teachings and what the Apostle Paul wrote in Galatians 6:9. It emphasizes that your actions determine the outcomes in your life and that you can either live a purposeful life aligned with God's will or find yourself in spiritual battles when living in sin.

4. **Abraham's Righteousness Through Faith and Action:** The example of Abraham is cited to illustrate the connection between faith and action. Abraham's faith was considered righteous because he not only believed but also acted upon his faith, such as offering his son Isaac on the altar. His faith and actions worked together.

5. **A Personal Story:** The message shares a personal story about a man who prayed for weight loss but didn't see results until he combined his faith with actions, such as eating healthier and exercising. This story illustrates that faith alone is not enough; actions are required to see significant changes.

6. **"Check Your Roots" Message:** The main motive of the message is encapsulated in the title, "Check Your Roots." It encourages readers to examine their faith and consider whether their faith is producing good works, as faith without works is described as dead.

7. **The Power of Faith Accompanied by Action:** The message concludes by emphasizing that faith accompanied by action can make the impossible possible, highlighting the importance of having a living and active faith.

8. **Closing Prayer:** The message ends with a prayer thanking God for the message and asking for the capacity to understand the importance of faith accompanied by works to walk in God's purpose.

Overall, this message underscores the importance of having faith that is accompanied by actions, using analogies, biblical examples, and a personal story to drive home the message that faith without works is lifeless.

Come And Follow Me

Jesus declared, "I am the way, the truth, and the life," as recorded in John 14:6 of the Bible. "No one comes to the father except through me." This implies that having a direct relationship with Jesus Christ, accepting Him as your Lord and Savior, and abiding by His teachings are the only ways to enter the gates of heaven. His death and resurrection have made it possible for us to receive forgiveness for our sins and a stamped boarding ticket for all eternity.

It's safe to say that your experience in heaven is based on how you live here on Earth!

This message is entitled, "Come and Follow Me"!

Following Jesus involves several aspects of one's life. Now if you're just starting your walk with Christ or even if you've been walking with Christ, I'm going to be fruitful and multiply and share a list of wisdom to help strengthen your roots while here on Earth.

The first topic I'm going to cover is "Believe and Have Faith." Trust in Jesus as the Son of God and believe in His death and resurrection for the forgiveness of sins. John 3:16-17 states, "For God so loved the world, that he gave his only Son, that whoever believes in him should not perish but have eternal life. For God did not send his Son into the world to condemn the world, but in order that the world might be saved through him." Romans 10:9 states, "If you confess with your mouth that Jesus is Lord and believe in your heart that God raised him from the dead, you will be saved." Believing is the key, ladies and gentlemen. Not just believing when everything is going great, but even believing and having faith in him when it seems your world is falling apart.

The next thing we are going to cover is "Repentance." Acts 3:19 reads, "Repent, therefore, and turn back, that your sins may be blotted out." Luke 24:47 reads, "And that repentance for the forgiveness of sins should be proclaimed in his name to all nations, beginning from Jerusalem." These verses emphasize how crucial repentance is to the Christian faith. Repentance is confessing and abdicating one's faults, pleading with God for forgiveness, and making an effort to live a life in accordance with His Word. It is a vital phase in obtaining God's forgiveness and going through spiritual transformation.

Our third topic is "Prayer." Maintain a regular and sincere prayer life, communicating with God, seeking His guidance, and expressing gratitude and praise. Philippians 4:6 reads, "Do not be anxious about anything, but in every situation, by prayer and petition, with thanksgiving, present your requests to God." 1 Thessalonians 5:16-18 states, "Rejoice always, pray continually, give thanks in all circumstances; for this is God's will for you in Christ Jesus." Colossians 4:2 says, "Devote yourselves to prayer, being watchful and thankful." As you can see, prayer is quite important in the biblical context. It is a way for us to communicate with God and make known to Him our feelings, ideas, and desires. We can ask for direction, comfort, and forgiveness through prayer. It helps us to better know God and to connect our hearts with His will. Through prayer, we can give our concerns and anxieties to God while putting our faith in His omnipotence and sovereignty. We can sense God's presence in our lives and grow closer to Him through this spiritual exercise. In the end, prayer is an effective tool that ties us to God and fortifies our faith.

Now onto the next topic, "Studying the Bible." Reading and studying the Scriptures help to understand God's teachings, His character, and how to live a life that pleases Him. Colossians 3:16 reads, "Let the message of Christ dwell among you richly as you teach and admonish one another with all wisdom through psalms, hymns, and songs from the Spirit, singing to God with gratitude in your hearts." 2 Timothy 3:16 says, "All Scripture is God-breathed and is useful for teaching, rebuking, correcting, and training in righteousness." These verses stress the value of studying and contemplating the Bible to acknowledge it as the divinely inspired Word of God. It leads, educates, and gives us the tools we need to live virtuously. We develop insight, discernment, and wisdom by immersing ourselves in the Scripture. We develop our understanding of God and His ways through the study of the Bible, allowing His Word to mold our attitudes, deeds, and character.

Topic number five is "Obeying His commandments." The Bible presents God's commandments as guidelines for righteous living and expressions of His perfect will. When we obey God's commandments, we demonstrate our love for Him and our desire to live in harmony with His divine plan. The Ten Commandments were given by God to the Israelites in the Old Testament as a moral code to direct their lives and forge a covenant relationship with Him. The different facets of life covered by these commandments include our interactions with God and other people. By following them, we respect life, protect marital faithfulness, honor our parents, and honor God. We also refrain from stealing, speaking falsely, coveting, and worshiping false gods. Jesus reaffirmed the significance of keeping God's commands in the New Testament. Two principles—loving God with all our heart, soul, and mind and loving our neighbor as ourselves were the essence of the Ten Commandments. According to what Jesus taught, love and confidence in Him can change a person's heart such that obedience comes naturally. Our lives are enriched and blessed when we are obedient to the Lord's instructions. Jesus said in John 14:15, "If you love me, keep my commands." Therefore, being obedient to God's commands is a manifestation of our love and devotion to God, rather than just fulfilling legal obligations.

On to number six, which is "Worship and Fellowship." Psalm 100:2 - "Worship the Lord with gladness; come before him with joyful songs John 4:23-24 - "Yet a time is coming and has now come when the true worshipers will worship the Father in the Spirit and in truth, for they are the kind of worshipers the Father seeks. God is spirit, and his worshipers must worship in the Spirit and in truth." Worship is the act of worshiping and honoring God with reverence. It entails expressing to Him our love, appreciation, and amazement. We recognize God's majesty, sovereignty, and deservingness through worship. We approach God through worship, giving Him our thanks, adoration, and submission. The fellowship enables us to find support and accountability in one another while also developing our spiritual growth. It offers a setting for education, instruction, and discipleship. Additionally, fellowship enables us to show love, care for one another, and represent Jesus to the outside world.

Now for the last topic, which is my personal favorite, "Sharing the Gospel" and spreading the good news of Jesus Christ with others. In Matthew 28:19-20, Jesus instructs His disciples to "go and make disciples of all nations, baptizing them in the name of the Father and of the Son and of the Holy Spirit, and teaching them to obey everything I have commanded you." This commission applies to all believers, urging them to share the gospel and make disciples. In all honesty, I'm not sure if there will ever come a day when I'm not talking about God. Throughout the years, I have been through a lot, but through it all, the Lord was always there to pick me up when I let myself fall. I recently spoke on a radio show, and I heard someone say that the greatest story you can ever tell is your testimony behind who you are today.

Friends, I don't know about you, but as I look back over my life, God has been faithful to me! I hope you can utilize the tools of today and be fruitful and multiply. Always remember that following Jesus is a lifelong journey of growing in faith, love, and obedience to Him.

Maybe you are someone reading and want to change the trajectory of your life. If so, then this prayer is for you.

Prayer:

Heavenly Father,

As we delve into the message of "Come and Follow Me," centered on the profound truth of Jesus as the way, the truth, and the life, we bow before You in gratitude. Your Word in John 14:6 echoes through our hearts, reminding us that a direct relationship with Jesus is the key to eternal life.

Lord Jesus, we acknowledge that our experience in heaven is indeed based on how we live here on Earth. We pray for the strength to follow You in every aspect of our lives. Today, we focus on the wisdom shared regarding our walk with Christ. Grant us the grace of genuine repentance. Enable us to confess our faults, seek Your forgiveness, and strive to live in accordance with Your Word. May repentance be a vital phase in our spiritual journey. In Jesus name we pray, Amen!

The key points of this message entitled "Come And Follow Me" are as follows:

1. **The Way to Heaven**: The devotional starts by emphasizing that Jesus declared Himself as "the way, the truth, and the life" and that no one can come to the Father except through Him. It underscores the importance of having a direct relationship with Jesus, accepting Him as Lord and Savior, and following His teachings for eternal salvation.

2. **Living on Earth Affects Your Heavenly Experience**: It suggests that one's experience in heaven is influenced by how one lives on Earth, emphasizing the significance of living a life aligned with Jesus' teachings.

3. **Seven Aspects of Following Jesus**: The message proceeds to cover seven aspects of following Jesus:
   - Believe and Have Faith- Emphasizes trusting in Jesus as the Son of God and believing in His death and resurrection for the forgiveness of sins.

   - Repentance- Highlights the importance of confessing faults, seeking forgiveness from God, and aligning one's life with His Word.

   - Prayer- Stresses the importance of maintaining a regular and sincere prayer life, seeking God's guidance, and expressing gratitude and praise.

- Studying the Bible- Encourages reading and studying the Scriptures to understand God's teachings, His character, and how to live a life that pleases Him.

- Obeying His Commandments- Discusses the significance of following God's commandments as guidelines for righteous living and expressions of His perfect will.

- Worship and Fellowship- Highlights the act of worshiping and honoring God with reverence and the importance of fellowship for support, accountability, and spiritual growth.

-Sharing the Gospel- Encourages spreading the good news of Jesus Christ with others and making disciples, as instructed by Jesus in Matthew 28:19-20.

4. **The Significance of Personal Testimony**: It emphasizes the importance of sharing one's personal testimony and how it can be a powerful tool for spreading the message of faith and transformation.
5. **The Lifelong Journey of Following Jesus**: The message closes by reminding readers that following Jesus is a lifelong journey of growing in faith, love, and obedience to Him.
6. **Closing Prayer**: The message ends with a prayer for those who may want to change the trajectory of their lives, asking for God's guidance and salvation.

Overall, this message collectively conveys the importance of faith, repentance, prayer, Scripture study, obedience, worship, fellowship, and sharing the gospel in one's journey of following Jesus and living a life that aligns with His teachings.

Divine Disruption

Life itself is full of disruptive situations! It could be the passing of a parent or spouse, the loss of a job, a move across the country, the arrival of a child, an unwelcome prognosis, or even an unforeseen global pandemic that puts the entirety of life on hold.

Believe it or not, the proper lens to look through when things like this are taking place simply means that God is doing something new.

This message is entitled "Divine Disruption."

Isaiah 43:19 says, "Behold, I will do a new thing, now it shall spring forth; shall you not know it? I will even make a road in the wilderness and rivers in the desert."

God is constantly starting things over. He promises His followers in this verse that He will carry out a "new thing" after rescuing them from Babylonian captivity.

Now, the phrase "new" in Hebrew is "Chadash". It speaks of something that has never occurred before or never existed. In the previous verse (Chapter 43:18), God says: "Forget the former things; do not dwell on the past."

As fellow Israelites, the Judeans had a long history of God performing wonderful miracles for them. They were the offspring of people who crossed the Red Sea on dry land when God created sea barriers. They were the kin of the people who drank water when Moses struck the rock.

These stories have been passed down through the decades to remind people of the God they served. These stories are what would have kept their optimism alive despite everything life may have thrown at them. These stories would probably also give them the strength to withstand their slavery in Babylon. However, God was giving them a fresh reason for hope.

God was warning them not to think too much about those old stories or to look back on them. God wants them to look ahead. He wished for them to base their hopes on what He would do for them in the future.

When the Israelites were set free from Babylonian captivity, they would have to walk through the wilderness to reach Judah. Now, that was not going to be simple for people who had just been freed from slavery. They would have to contend with wide-open spaces, hot, dry, and dusty ground, and limited vegetation. They would have to contend with hazardous reptiles like snakes, fight wild animals, they'd lack food and water, and would have to battle a plethora of nations that may attack them.

When the Israelites were fleeing Egypt, God had previously performed something for them. However, this time would be unique. God would do it in a way that they could never have imagined.

And that takes us back to our opening scripture (Isaiah 43:19): "Behold, I will do a new thing, now it shall spring forth; shall you not know it?"

Maybe the same miracle God did for them, He's performing in your life. But you're so used to it happening the same way, you continuously remind yourself of all the old ways He got you through it!

But what if I told you that this time it's going to come in a different form than usual... this time it's going to lead you on a different path than usual... This time God may use new people, end up placing you in a foreign environment, or place you in situations that make you uncomfortable... this time it's going to take divine disruption.

If we take a seedling, for example, for that little seed to become the fruit-bearing tree that we benefit from, there first must be the disruption and breakage of the soil to impart that seed.

For the birthing of a baby, there first must be disruption and painful labor from the mother's womb in order to finally see your bundle of joy.

Here's another one. When you're in the gym working out and trying to gain muscle mass, there first must be the tearing and breakage of the muscle to see the results you so desperately covet.

Friends, I for one can tell you that if you want change, then you will first have to endure some type of disruption. As a matter of fact, that is just a part of God's process for your growth. So, if you're not willing to encounter disruption, then stop praying for change.

"Behold, I will do a new thing, now it shall spring forth; shall you not know it?"

Prayer:

Heavenly Father,

As we gather in prayer, we recognize the truth embedded in the message of "Divine Disruption." Life, at times, brings forth unexpected challenges, disruptions that may seem overwhelming. Yet, we trust in Your promise from Isaiah 43:19, declaring that You are doing a new thing.

Lord, open our hearts to understand that these disruptions are not meant to discourage us but to usher in a fresh start, a new beginning orchestrated by Your divine hand. Help us embrace the concept of "Chadash," something entirely new and unprecedented, breaking away from the patterns of the past.

As we reflect on the history of the Israelites, remind us, Lord, that looking forward is essential. Guide us to place our hope in Your future plans rather than dwelling on past miracles. Grant us the courage to trust You as we navigate through the wilderness of change, knowing that Your ways are beyond our comprehension. Lord, if there are areas in our lives where we resist disruption, give us the strength to surrender to Your divine plan. In Jesus name we pray, Amen!

The key points of this message entitled "Divine Disruption" are as follows:

1. **Life's Disruptions**: The message acknowledges that life is filled with disruptive situations, which can include the loss of loved ones, job loss, relocation, unexpected challenges, and global events like a pandemic. These disruptions can be unsettling and challenging.

2. **God's Promise of Something New**: The message draws from Isaiah 43:19, emphasizing that God promises to do something new. The Hebrew word "chadash" denotes something that has never occurred before. It suggests that God is constantly initiating new things in the lives of His followers.

3. **Letting Go of the Past**: The message references Isaiah 43:18, where God instructs His people not to dwell on the past but to focus on what He will do in the future. This encourages readers to let go of past experiences and look forward with hope.

4. **The Wilderness Metaphor**: The Israelites' journey through the wilderness after their release from Babylonian captivity is used as a metaphor. The wilderness represents a challenging and unfamiliar terrain filled with various hardships.

5. **Expecting a New Miracle**: The message highlights that, just as God had performed miracles for the Israelites in the past, He was going to do something new for them in their journey through the wilderness. This emphasizes the concept of divine disruption.

6. **Change Through Disruption**: The message suggests that change often requires disruption. It uses examples like the breaking of soil for seedlings to grow, the labor pains of

childbirth, and the tearing of muscle fibers during workouts to illustrate how disruption can lead to growth and change.

7. **Embracing Divine Disruption**: Divine disruption is a part of God's process for growth and change in a person's life. It encourages readers to embrace disruption to achieve the change they desire and to stop praying for change if they are not willing to endure disruption.

8. **Closing Prayer**: The message concludes with a prayer thanking God for the message and asking for guidance and strength to embrace divine disruption in one's life.

Overall, this message emphasizes the idea that disruptions in life can lead to something new and transformative, especially when guided by faith in God's plan. It encourages readers to have a forward-looking perspective and to be open to the ways in which God may bring change and blessings, even if it involves discomfort and disruption.

Don't Give Up

In the book of Galatians, the Apostle Paul communicates, "Let us not become weary in doing good, for at the proper time, we will reap a harvest if we do not give up." Paul encourages Christians in this passage of Scripture not to become weary in doing good.

It can be challenging to resist getting worn out when doing good, yet God does not want us to. God wants us to keep doing things righteously and enlighten the world with His shining light.

This message is entitled "Don't Give Up!"

God promises to all believers that if they remain strong and continue doing good, they will reap a harvest at the appropriate time, and they shouldn't grow tired of doing good.

Paul knew that the Galatian church was burdened by the duties of daily Christian living when he addressed this epistle.

Perhaps you have experienced this feeling before.

Perhaps you know what it's like to wake up every morning and proclaim that for Christ, I live and for Christ, I die and strive to do good work for the kingdom.

Paul urges them not to give up on doing good to lift their spirits and encourage them.

Although living as a Christian is challenging, we have the support of the Holy Spirit. Every day, he will assist, support, and encourage us.

The Holy Spirit is always available and willing to lift us. He can help us in choosing the path of righteousness over the path of the flesh.

Using myself as an example here… I enjoy teaching the word. Teaching the word of God is a form of doing good. That's certainly what the Apostle Paul was encouraging Timothy in 2 Timothy 4:2 when he says: "Preach the word! Be ready in season and out of season. Convince, rebuke, exhort, with all long-suffering and teaching."

Paul says, "Teach the Word when it's welcomed; teach it when it's not welcomed." The teaching of the Word is certainly the joyous task of the church. But not just the church confined between four walls, but also in reference to the body.

Preaching and teaching the Bible is unquestionably beneficial. It is my Divine duty and joyful responsibility. But it is also my job to be prepared to impart the Word. It must be done not just through what I say, but by the way I love people and live my everyday life!

However, it's not always a simple task. There will be challenging times and periods when the teaching of the Bible will be opposed. It's possible that I'll face vast amounts of harsh criticism. There will be moments when I might not have other people's support while doing good.

Or I might be tempted to try to carry out the good deed on my own, not fully relying on God for the ability and knowledge to carry it out through his power.

The temptation to give up is always present when things are difficult or tough. Furthermore, when the fruit and the harvest of the church's good works are frequently delayed, there is always a temptation to give up.

When this happens, I remember the words of Paul in 1 Corinthians 15:58. "Therefore, my beloved brethren, be steadfast, immovable, always abounding in the work of the Lord, knowing that your labor is not in vain in the Lord."

Your life may not be what it should be right now, but if you keep going and look to God and fulfill His purpose for your life, it can be.

Friends, whatever your "doing good" is... Turn to God if you are feeling worn out and tired from it. He has the power to raise you up. Remember that whatever you are working on, you are working for the Lord whenever you feel worn out, disappointed, or depressed. You are serving the Lord Jesus Christ. God is aware of all the good things, nice words, and deeds you commit.

Nothing you do escapes the notice of our Heavenly Father. As stated in Hebrews, "God is not unjust; he will not forget your work and the love you have shown him as you have helped his people and continue to help them." You are serving the Lord; you are not serving men. Never lose sight of this essential fact, and never stop doing good. Your work is being acknowledged.

You may have experienced conflict or difficult times in your personal life, your church, your place of employment, or your academic career. You're exhausted because of it. The encouraging message is to persevere. Why? Because a harvest will be produced. God will provide for us. When? In due season. It might happen in this life, or it might not. Some diligent workers produce few results in this life. However, the harvest will undoubtedly occur throughout the fullness of the kingdom.

This message is one of hope. Your efforts are not in vain. God is dependable and will offer us a harvest of blessings despite our challenges.

Therefore, resist the urge to quit and take a back seat because of life's challenges. Keep your Christian faith strong and moving forward. And continue serving others and doing good deeds, just like Paul said...

We will reap a harvest at the proper time if we do not give up.

Jonathyn J. Williams

Prayer:

Heavenly Father,

We come before you with grateful hearts, acknowledging your guidance and wisdom in our lives. Thank you for the timely message that encourages us not to give up in doing good, especially when faced with challenges and weariness.

Lord, we lift up our struggles and moments of exhaustion to you. Your Word reminds us not to grow weary in doing good, for in due season, we will reap a harvest if we do not give up. Strengthen our resolve, O Lord, to persevere in the path of righteousness, even when the journey becomes difficult.

We pray for those who may be feeling worn out, discouraged, or tempted to give up on doing good. Pour out your Holy Spirit upon them, providing the strength and endurance needed to continue in faith. May they find encouragement in knowing that their labor is not in vain in you, O Lord.

Just as the Apostle Paul encouraged the Galatians, we seek your guidance to stay steadfast and immovable in our commitment to doing good. Grant us the grace to abound in the work of the Lord, knowing that our service is ultimately unto you, our Heavenly Father. In Jesus name I pray, Amen!

The key points of this message entitled "Don't Give Up" are as follows:

1. **Scriptural Inspiration**: The message draws inspiration from the book of Galatians, where the Apostle Paul encourages Christians not to become weary in doing good, emphasizing that they will reap a harvest if they do not give up.
2. **Perseverance in Doing Good**: It highlights the importance of not getting worn out when doing good deeds and living a righteous life. The message is to continue serving God faithfully and positively influencing the world.

3. **Challenges in Christian Living**: The message acknowledges that living as a Christian can be challenging, but it reminds readers that they have the support of the Holy Spirit to assist and encourage them in their journey.

4. **Examples of Doing Good**: It uses the example of teaching the Word of God as a form of doing good and emphasizes the importance of being prepared to impart the Word both in words and actions.

5. **Facing Opposition and Criticism**: The message acknowledges that there will be opposition, criticism, and moments when support might be lacking when doing good deeds. It urges readers not to give in to the temptation to give up.

6. **Hope and Encouragement**: The message provides hope by citing 1 Corinthians 15:58, which encourages steadfastness and immovability in the work of the Lord, with the promise that their labor is not in vain.

7. **Recognition from God**: It reminds readers that God notices and appreciates their good deeds, quoting Hebrews to emphasize that God does not forget their work and love shown to His people.

8. **Perseverance and Harvest**: The core message is one of hope and perseverance, emphasizing that a harvest of blessings will come at the proper time if individuals do not give up on doing good.

9. **Prayer**: The message closes with a prayer, asking God to provide rest, strength, and guidance for the week ahead, enabling believers to continue doing good and serving others.

Overall, this message encourages readers to remain steadfast in their commitment to doing good and serving God, even in the face of challenges and opposition, with the assurance that their efforts will ultimately yield a harvest of blessings.

Finish Strong

Life's challenges can oftentimes make us lose focus and grow weary. However, the Bible calls us to persevere and remain faithful until the end. Let's delve into the Scriptures so that we can obtain a comprehensive understanding of how we can finish strong and fulfill God's purposes for our lives.

This message is entitled "Finish Strong."

Throughout the Bible, we are reminded of the importance of perseverance. In Hebrews 12:1, the apostle Paul encourages us to run the race with endurance, not being swayed by obstacles or setbacks. In Matthew 24:13, Jesus Himself reassures us that those who endure to the end will be saved. The call to finish strong is a recurring theme that highlights the significance of remaining steadfast in our faith.

Every task or endeavor we undertake has a purpose. When we finish what we start, we align ourselves with God's plans for our lives. God has uniquely designed each of us with gifts, talents, and opportunities to serve Him and others. By finishing well, we honor God and fulfill the purposes He has for us.

Joseph's life in the Book of Genesis is an incredible story of perseverance. From being sold into slavery by his brothers to being wrongly imprisoned, Joseph faced numerous setbacks. However, he remained faithful to the Lord and used his God-given gifts of interpretation to rise to a position of authority in Egypt. In the end, Joseph's perseverance led to the reconciliation of his family and the fulfillment of God's plan.

The apostle Paul is a prominent example of perseverance in the New Testament. Throughout his ministry, Paul encountered numerous trials, including beatings, imprisonments, and shipwrecks. Despite these challenges, he remained steadfast in his faith, boldly proclaiming the Gospel and establishing churches. Paul's perseverance is evident in his words in 2 Timothy 4:7, where he declares, "I have fought the good fight, I have finished the race, have kept the faith."

I don't know about you, but when I commit to a task or project, whether to myself or to others, it is important that I follow through. Finishing what you started demonstrates your trustworthiness and reliability. It shows that you value your word and take responsibility for your actions. Honoring your commitments strengthens your relationships and builds trust with others.

I've learned that actions speak louder than words, and by finishing what we start, we set a positive example for those around us. Whether it's our family, friends, colleagues, or fellow believers, our perseverance and determination inspire others to do the same. We can encourage others to persevere by showing them the value of completing what we've set out to do.

Friends, always step up and finish strong! By doing this, we align ourselves with God's purposes, develop character and discipline, gain a sense of accomplishment, honor our commitments, and set a positive example for others. Let us strive to be individuals who persevere, not only for our own benefit but also for the glory of God and the encouragement of those around us.

Prayer:

Heavenly Father,

As we come before You, we acknowledge Your sovereignty and seek Your guidance in our journey of faith. We thank You for the encouragement and wisdom found in Your Word regarding the call to finish strong.

Grant us the endurance and perseverance to run the race You have set before us, just as the apostle Paul urged in Hebrews 12:1. Help us navigate through life's challenges and obstacles, keeping our focus on You.

In Matthew 24:13, Jesus reassures us that those who endure to the end will be saved. Strengthen our hearts, Lord, so that we may endure and remain faithful until the completion of the race set before us.

As we reflect on the stories of Joseph and the apostle Paul, may their examples inspire us to trust in Your plans and remain steadfast in our faith. Just as Paul declared, "I have fought the good fight, I have finished the race, I have kept the faith" (2 Timothy 4:7), may we also finish strong in our journey with You.

Lord, instill in us the importance of finishing what we start. Help us to honor our commitments, be reliable and trustworthy, and demonstrate the values of discipline and determination. May our actions speak louder than words, setting a positive example for those around us. In Jesus name we pray, Amen!

The key points of this message entitled "Finish Strong" are as follows:

- **Life's Challenges and Perseverance**: Life's challenges can make us lose focus and grow weary, but the Bible encourages us to persevere and remain faithful until the end.
- **Biblical References**: The message references Hebrews 12:1, where the apostle Paul encourages us to run the race with endurance, and Matthew 24:13, where Jesus reassures us that those who endure to the end will be saved. The call to finish strong is a recurring theme in the Bible.
- **Purpose and Alignment with God's Plans**: Every task or endeavor we undertake has a purpose, and when we finish what we start, we align ourselves with God's plans for our lives.
- **Examples from Scripture**: The message cites examples from Scripture, such as Joseph in the Book of Genesis and the apostle Paul in the New Testament, who demonstrated perseverance

and ultimately fulfilled God's purposes despite facing setbacks and challenges.

- **Honoring Commitments and Building Trust**: Finishing what we start demonstrates trustworthiness, reliability, and a commitment to our word. It strengthens relationships and builds trust with others.
- **Setting a Positive Example**: Actions speak louder than words, and by finishing what we start, we set a positive example for those around us, inspiring them to persevere in their own endeavors.
- **Alignment with God's Purposes**: Finishing strong aligns us with God's purposes, helps develop character and discipline, and brings a sense of accomplishment.
- **Encouragement and Prayer**: The message encourages readers to step up and finish strong, seeking God's protection from distractions and temptations. It includes a prayer asking for discernment, passion for purpose, and inspiration for those who may be considering giving up on their goals.

Overall, this message highlights the importance of perseverance, aligning with God's plans, and setting a positive example for others by finishing what we start. It encourages readers to honor their commitments and seek inspiration and strength from God to finish strong in their pursuits.

Grow Where You're Planted

I want to take a moment to delve into the Gospel of St. Luke! Luke is the third of the four storytellers of the life of Jesus in the New Testament. Through the lens of his perspective, Luke's Gospel encourages us to spend more time reflecting on the character of Jesus and his life, ministry, teachings, death, burial, resurrection, and ascension. Today's teaching aims to show you how to live purposefully now, so you can live in a more abundant way in the future.

This message is entitled "Grow Where You're Planted."

Jesus said to his disciples in Luke 16:10, "Whoever is faithful in very little is also faithful in much, and whoever is unrighteous in very little is also unrighteous in much. So, who will trust you with what is genuine if you have not been faithful with worldly wealth? And if you have not been faithful with what belongs to someone else, who will give you what is your own?"

Jesus makes it quite plain when he instructs us to use our earnings and material assets for the greater good. Such items exist to leave an eternal mark on the lives of others. If we are unfaithful with the material possessions and riches we have been given in this life, we will also be unfaithful with the real riches promised to us in the afterlife. Christians must demonstrate our faith in God through our finances, belongings, and material goods. Our duty is to show the rest of the world that we value God above all else. It's safe to say that we are to grow where we are planted.

Friends, how can we expect the Lord to entrust us with much if we cannot be faithful over the little? Believe it or not, your stewardship and loyalty over the season that you are currently in will determine what your "much" is later. This verse is very relevant. God will be pleased with us in a significant matter if we can please Him in a modest matter. God surveys the heart of man on a deep level. The Lord will protect us so that we are able to stand firm in the big things if we are willing to remain faithful in small things, even when it seems impossible at times.

People often see the big-time events as being the very important ones, and they consider only those to be sent by God. Believe it or not, small events hold as much importance as the big ones, so never look down on a moment because God can use anything and anyone at any time to do what he wants to do throughout your life. Remember that life here on Earth is simply a mission. We are to make the best out of every aspect of this mission until it is time to return home.

Zechariah 4:10 says, "Do not despise these small beginnings, for the LORD rejoices to see the work begin." Remember that great things come out of small places, and always stay loyal to your small place. There is more fruit in the small places because it is your starting point and your molding point. It's so easy to become discouraged when you look around and see people living in the "much" when you are still living in the "little". Keep in mind that it's not a competition. We are not competing to say whose "much" is better than whose. This is simply about being faithful to where God has planted you while watering and nurturing your "little" until God says Yes! So, remain faithful to that small business, remain faithful to that tiny apartment, remain faithful to community college, remain faithful to that $15 in your bank account, and remain faithful to the little things so that in due season, The Lord can entrust you with much. You must grow where you're planted!

Prayer:

Heavenly Father,

We come before You with gratitude for the wisdom found in Your Word, specifically in the Gospel of St. Luke. Thank you for the teachings that guide us on how to live purposefully in the present and prepare for an abundant future.

As we reflect on the words of Jesus in Luke 16:10, we are reminded of the importance of faithfulness in both the little and much. Help us, Lord, to be faithful stewards of the resources, possessions, and opportunities You have entrusted to us. May our actions with worldly wealth reflect our devotion to You and our desire to leave an eternal mark on the lives of others.

Grant us the strength to grow where we are planted. In times when the tasks seem small or the resources seem limited, may we remain faithful, knowing that our stewardship in the little things determines the trust You place in us for the greater things.

Lord, help us not to despise small beginnings, for Your Word tells us that You rejoice to see the work begin (Zechariah 4:10). Give us the patience and perseverance to water and nurture the "little" aspects of our lives, understanding that great things can emerge from humble beginnings. In Jesus name we pray, Amen!

The key points of this message entitled "Grow Where You're Planted," are as follows:

1. **Reflection on Luke's Gospel:** The message encourages reflection on the character of Jesus and his life, ministry, teachings, death, burial, resurrection, and ascension as portrayed in the Gospel of Luke.
2. **Importance of Faithfulness:** The message emphasizes Jesus' teaching from Luke 16:10, which stresses the importance of being faithful in both small and large matters.
3. **Using Material Blessings for Good**: It encourages the use of one's earnings and material assets for the greater good and to make an eternal impact on the lives of others.
4. **Demonstrating Faith in God:** As Christians, it's suggested that we demonstrate our faith in God through our finances

and material possessions, showcasing that we value God above all else.

5. **The Significance of Small Beginnings:** The message reminds readers not to despise small beginnings and highlights that great things can come from seemingly insignificant places.

6. **Remaining Faithful in Your Current Season:** It emphasizes the importance of remaining faithful in one's current circumstances, regardless of how small or challenging they may seem, as it can shape what blessings come in the future.

7. **Understanding Life's Mission:** Life on Earth is framed as a mission, and individuals are encouraged to make the best of every aspect of this mission.

8. **Avoiding Comparison:** It discourages the urge to compare one's progress or blessings with others and emphasizes that faithfulness to one's current situation is the focus.

9. **The Power of Faith and Purpose:** The message concludes with a prayer that acknowledges the significance of "the little" in one's journey of faith and purpose, and it encourages readers to grow where they are planted.

Overall, these key points inclusively convey the essence of remaining faithful and purposeful in one's current circumstances, trusting that such faithfulness will lead to greater blessings in the future.

I Believe

"Everything is possible for one who believes." These profound words made by Jesus in Mark 9:23 capture the essence of firm faith and the limitless possibilities of belief. Jesus delivers a timeless truth in this brief but deep speech that resonates through the ages and speaks to the core of human existence.

The Christian doctrine is deeply entwined with the concept of belief. The foundation of our faith in the sovereignty of God, and His capacity to perform miracles in our lives is an essential aspect of our spiritual journey. Believing in God and His promises with all our hearts allows us to go beyond the boundaries of our limited perspective and step into the limitless opportunities that He can provide.

Join me as I decompress the essence of believing and how you should use it as you journey here on earth.

This message is entitled "I Believe".

In the life of a believer, the words "I believe" have great significance. They are a firm proclamation of our faith and confidence in the omnipotence of the Lord. By believing, we acknowledge that God is not constrained by the laws of this world and is able to perform incredible miracles that defy logic and explanation on behalf of humanity.

The ideology of believing keeps us going through difficult times in life. It gives us hope and strengthens our souls. Believing demonstrates our unshakable faith in God's ability to transform and rejuvenate our lives. It keeps us going when we face obstacles that appear insurmountable because we know just as St. Luke declared, "For with God, nothing shall be impossible" (Luke 1:37).

In the book of Mark, John Mark shares the parable about the woman with the issue of blood. In the story told in this passage, a lady who had been bleeding for twelve years reached out to touch Jesus' garment out of faith, believing that doing so would heal her.

The story reads, "Now a woman suffering from bleeding for twelve years had endured much under many doctors. She had spent everything she had and was not helped at all. On the contrary, she became worse. Having heard about Jesus, she came up behind him in the crowd and touched his clothing. For she said, "If I just touch his clothes, I'll be made well." Instantly her flow of blood ceased, and she sensed in her body that she was healed of her affliction. Immediately Jesus realized that power had gone out from him. He turned around in the crowd and said, "Who touched my clothes?" His disciples said to him, "You see the crowd pressing against you, and yet you say, 'Who touched me?'" But he was looking around to see who had done this. The woman, with fear and trembling, knowing what had happened to her, came and fell down before him and told him the whole truth. "Daughter," he said to her, "your faith has saved you. Go in peace and be healed from your affliction."

What I want you all to make note of in this story is that Jesus didn't necessarily move mountains or part the Red Sea for the lady to be healed. He said, "Your faith has saved you." Which means because she had faith in who the Son of God was and believed that he is who he says he is, that was enough.

Friends sometimes all God wants you to do is believe, but this belief has to be beyond human logic. In verse 26 it said that the woman "had endured much under many doctors," which means there wasn't anything they could do to help her. That's when she knew she had to go to Jesus because he can make a way out of no way and conquer what has not yet been seen in the eyes of humanity.

Now, believing isn't a one-time thing. You can believe for something and live in the expectation that it will show up tomorrow just because you asked for it. Remember the woman had the issue of blood for twelve years (Verse 25). Understand that believing can be a hard task to fulfill when living in the atmosphere of turmoil and affliction. I, for one, can tell you that It's tough to believe when you fail an exam. It's tough to believe when you receive more bills in the mail than checks a month. It's tough to believe when all hell is breaking loose and it seems that everything is going wrong, but even when you can't see it, you still have to believe. Remember this belief is not in yourself, but in the power of the true and living God!

So let me ask you… Do you believe? If so, then I'm joyful for you, but if not, then it's time to start today!

As we consider Mark 9:23's deep words, let us embrace the importance of belief in our day-to-day relationship with God. Let us firmly proclaim, "I believe," and establish ourselves in the unshakeable reality that, because of our believing, God's kindness and grace are abundant. May your lives be infused with the supernatural power of believing, enabling you to see the transforming and amazing work of our Heavenly Father.

Prayer:

Heavenly Father,

We come before You with hearts open to the message of "I Believe." Lord, help us grasp the profound truth in the words of Jesus, "Everything is possible for one who believes." Strengthen our faith and confidence in Your omnipotence, acknowledging that You are not constrained by the laws of this world.

We recognize the significance of the words "I believe" in the life of a believer. It is a proclamation of our faith and confidence in Your ability to perform incredible miracles. As we journey through life, let our belief in You be unwavering, providing hope and strengthening our souls.

We reflect on the story of the woman with the issue of blood, who, in her belief, reached out to touch Jesus' garment, trusting in the healing power. Lord, may we learn from her example that even in the face of seemingly insurmountable obstacles, our belief in You can bring about transformation.

We acknowledge that belief is not a one-time event but an ongoing expression of trust in Your power. Even in challenging times, when circumstances may seem overwhelming, help us to believe beyond human logic, knowing that You can make a way where there seems to be no way.

We declare, "I believe," not in ourselves but in the power of the true and living God. For those who may struggle with belief, Lord, ignite in their hearts a fresh faith and a newfound confidence in Your promises. In Jesus name we pray, Amen!

The key points of this message entitled "I Believe" are as follows:

1. **Foundation of Christian Faith:** The message emphasizes the deep connection between the Christian doctrine and the concept of belief. Belief in the sovereignty of God and His ability to perform miracles is considered essential in the spiritual journey.

2. **The Power of Belief:** The central theme revolves around the profound words of Jesus in Mark 9:23, stating that "everything is possible for one who believes." Believing in God and His promises is portrayed as a way to go beyond human limitations and access limitless opportunities.

3. **Significance of "I Believe":** The phrase "I believe" holds great significance in the life of a believer, representing a firm proclamation of faith and confidence in the omnipotence of the Lord.

4. **Faith in Action:** The message discusses the story of the woman with the issue of blood from the book of Mark. Her act of reaching out to touch Jesus' garment, fueled by faith, resulted

in her healing. The emphasis is on the transformative power of faith, even in situations that seem insurmountable.

5. **Belief Beyond Human Logic:** The narrative underscores that belief goes beyond human logic and understanding. The woman with the issue of blood had endured much under many doctors, but it was her faith in Jesus that ultimately brought about her healing.

6. **Persistence in Belief:** Believing is presented as an ongoing process, not a one-time event. Despite challenges and afflictions, the message encourages believers to persist in their faith, even when circumstances are tough.

7. **The Role of Belief in God's Work:** The message highlights that, in the story of the woman with the issue of blood, Jesus attributed her healing to her faith. This underscores the idea that sometimes all God requires is for individuals to believe in His power.

8. **Encouragement to Believe:** The message concludes with a question, "Do you believe?" and encourages readers to embrace belief in God's power, acknowledging that belief goes beyond oneself and is rooted in the power of the true and living God.

9. **Prayer for Strengthened Faith:** The message ends with a prayer, expressing gratitude for the message received and seeking God's help in overcoming doubts and fears. It asks for wisdom to trust in God's plan and for confidence to walk in the path set by Him.

10. **Call to Embrace Belief Daily:** The message calls for a daily embrace of belief, encouraging believers to firmly proclaim "I believe" and to establish themselves in the unshakeable reality that God's kindness and grace abound through belief.

The overall of this message is centered on the transformative power of belief in the context of Christian faith. It highlights the significance of faith and confidence in God's ability to perform miracles and emphasizes that everything is possible for those who believe. The narrative draws on the biblical story of the woman with the issue of blood to illustrate how unwavering belief can lead to healing and transformation, even in the face of seemingly insurmountable challenges. The devotional encourages believers to persist in their faith, even during difficult times, and underscores the idea that God may require nothing more than genuine belief in His power. The conclusion invites readers to daily embrace the proclamation "I believe" and to recognize the abundant kindness and grace that result from such belief in the journey of a Christian's relationship with God. The prayer at the end seeks strength in faith, wisdom to overcome doubt, and confidence to trust in God's divine plan.

I Have A Plan

_____

Jeremiah 29:11 reads, "For I know the plans I have for you, declares the Lord, plans to prosper you and not to harm you, plans to give you hope and a future."

This message is entitled "I Have A Plan."

Jeremiah was a prophet who lived in the final days before Judah was exiled by the Babylonians. He continued to function in that capacity for a large portion of the time that the Jews were in exile. The prophecies that Jeremiah received from God throughout his ministry are brought together in the book of Jeremiah.

These were Jeremiah's comments to the Jews who had lived under the rule of the Egyptian and then the Babylonian Empires before being exiled from Jerusalem to Babylon. One can only imagine living under the rule of one's enemies and then being compelled to flee your country and make a new life abroad by your adversaries.

Now, in the previous chapter, Jeremiah had just recently handed down judgment on the false prophet Hananiah. Hananiah had promised the people that God would lift their captivity in Babylon within two years, allowing them to return home. Although the people probably found his speech persuasive, it was a lie that caused God to wipe Hananiah off the face of the Earth (Jeremiah 28:15–17).

Instead, Jeremiah warns the people that they would have to spend at least 70 years in Babylon. To ensure the peace and prosperity of the city where they now found themselves, they should settle down, construct homes, get married, and pray for peace while doing so (Jeremiah 29:4–10).

We learn that Jeremiah 29:11 was addressed to individuals who were having trouble and suffering, people who perhaps desired a quick rescue like the one Hananiah falsely claimed to have. However, God's response isn't to provide an immediate escape from the problematic circumstance. Instead, God assures them that despite their predicament, He has a plan to prosper them.

Believe it or not, God still connects with us through a promise he gave to the people while in exile. We may confidently apply the essence of this promise to our lives right now if we have a clear understanding of the nature of God's plans for us as followers of Christ and the foundation of the good he promises to us today.

We now understand that it is not a promise to save us from adversity or suffering right away but rather a promise that God has a plan for our life and that He can use whatever is going on right now to benefit us and deliver us a brighter future.

In my opinion, the refuge that the Lord is providing through this dialogue holds even more comfort because God tells Jeremiah immediately in the following verses that if one were to "call on me and come and pray to me... I will listen to you. You will seek me and find me when you seek me with all your heart" (Jeremiah 19:12–13).

Friends, we can only imagine how much faith was needed for the people of that time to be exercised daily to stay content in Babylon. As a matter of fact, it's safe to say that they are stuck in their preparation phase or what I personally like to call God's Waiting Room.

Now going back to Jeremiah 29:11, sometimes we can tend to get impatient with God through the process, and in doing that, we start to abandon His plan for our lives. You feel that you shouldn't have to go through what you're going through as long as you've been going through it, and you find yourself in a season where you're now demanding immediate rescue from your preparation.

You're looking at everyone else's lives, and then start to observe yours and make a self-diagnosis that what you're going through is too tough and that God is done with you, and I just want to remind you today, friends, that God's timing is the right timing.

And I believe that that's a word for somebody today. You've been walking through life without clarity and feel that you have little purpose and no hope. And I just want you to know that in due season God has plans to prosper you and to give you hope and a promising future.

Prayer:

Heavenly Father,

As we come before you today, we are grateful for the assurance and promise found in Your Word. Jeremiah 29:11 reminds us that You have plans for us, plans to prosper us and not to harm us, plans to give us hope and a future. In moments of trouble and uncertainty, we find comfort in knowing that Your plans for us are filled with goodness and purpose.

We acknowledge the historical context of this scripture, where Your people faced adversity and exile. Yet, your response was not immediate rescue but a promise of a brighter future. Today, we hold on to this promise, recognizing that Your plans unfold in Your perfect timing.

Lord, help us to exercise faith daily, especially when we find ourselves in what may feel like Your Waiting Room. Grant us patience to endure the process, knowing that Your timing is the right timing. In moments of impatience, help us to trust in Your sovereignty and wisdom.

We lift up those who may be struggling in seasons of waiting, feeling discouraged and questioning their purpose. Remind them, Lord, that Your plans are not abandoned, and Your timing is always perfect. May they find hope in the promise of a prosperous and promising future. In Jesus name we pray, Amen!

The key points of this message entitled "I Have A Plan" are as follows:

- **Scriptural Foundation**: The message begins with a quote from Jeremiah 29:11, emphasizing that God knows the plans He has for individuals, plans for prosperity, hope, and a future.
- **Context of Jeremiah**: It provides some context about Jeremiah, a prophet who delivered messages to the Jewish people during the time of their exile in Babylon. The people faced adversity and uncertainty in a foreign land.
- **False Promises and God's Response**: It mentions the false promise of a quick rescue from exile made by the false prophet Hananiah, which led to his judgment. Instead, Jeremiah warned the people that they would spend at least 70 years in Babylon and encouraged them to settle down, build homes, and pray for peace in their new circumstances.
- **God's Plan Amidst Adversity**: The message emphasizes that God's response to the people's suffering was not an immediate escape from their situation but a promise that He had a plan for their lives. It underscores that God can use current challenges to shape a brighter future.
- **Application to Modern Life**: It encourages readers to apply the essence of Jeremiah 29:11 to their lives, understanding that God's plans may not always involve an instant removal of difficulties but a purposeful journey towards a better future.
- **Seeking God with All One's Heart**: The message points out the importance of seeking God with sincerity and wholeheartedness, emphasizing that God listens to those who call upon Him.
- **God's Waiting Room**: It likens the period of waiting and preparation to "God's Waiting Room," where individuals may feel impatient or demand immediate rescue from their circumstances.

- **God's Timing**: The central message is about patience and trust in God's timing. It reminds readers that God's timing is always right, even when life seems unclear or challenging.
- **Hope and Promising Future**: The message concludes with a message of hope, reassuring readers that, in due season, God plans to prosper them and provide a promising future.
- **Prayer**: The message ends with a prayer expressing gratitude to God for the message and asking for faith, hope, and patience in His plan.

Overall, this message encourages readers to trust in God's plan for their lives, even when faced with difficulties and uncertainties, and to remember that God's timing is perfect. It emphasizes the importance of seeking God wholeheartedly and finding hope in the promise of a prosperous and hopeful future.

It's Time To Go

The act of leaving behind the familiar teaches us a valuable lesson regarding faith. It reminds us that when God calls us to do a certain thing, he often requires us to step out of our comfort zones and trust in his guidance. In this moment, I want to delve into the book of Genesis and walk with Abraham (who was once Abram) as he reflects on what it truly means to step out in obedience and walk the journey of hope.

This message is entitled "It's Time To Go."

The trust and obedience of Abram, the man who would eventually be called Abraham, are shown here in the book of Genesis. Abram heard from God, who gave him the order to travel to an unknown land and leave behind everything he knew. Abram had to leave behind his father's house, his family, and even his country to fulfill this supernatural calling of the Lord.

Genesis 12 reads, "The Lord had said to Abram, 'Go from your country, your people and your father's household to the land I will show you.' 2 'I will make you into a great nation, and I will bless you. I will make your name great, and you will be a blessing. 3 I will bless those who bless you, and whoever curses you I will curse; and all peoples on earth will be blessed through you.'"

Now, the name Abram is masculine and of Akkadian descent. In far later languages, it is translated as "exalted father."

The name "Abraham" means "father of a multitude" or "father of many nations." This change in name represents the fulfillment of God's promise to provide Abraham with many descendants who would go on to become powerful nations. It represents the position and destiny that God had planned for him in the future.

The name change from Abram to Abraham signifies a shift in focus, from being a man with a personal legacy to becoming a vessel through which God's redemptive plan for humanity would be realized. It is a testament to Abraham's faith and obedience as he embraced his new name and the purpose for which God had called him.

Now, understand something! He arrived as Abram, but he departed as Abraham. As I studied this text, the wisdom I gained was that the Abraham of the new could not become the father of many nations if he stayed as Abram of the old. If you go back to the scripture, the first command that the Lord gave Abram was to leave everything he knew and was comfortable with. This means that the magnitude of what the Lord had planned for his life required him to let go of what was in order to step into his written destiny. Abram acknowledged that it was time to go!

You know, Genesis 12 is my personal favorite of all the Bible because I feel that I relate to the dialogue in a plethora of ways. I was born and raised in Dallas, Texas. I remember when I received my call to ministry; I thought that I'd live my entire life in Dallas, and that it was the city the Lord wanted me to build his kingdom in. About 7 months went by, and I felt as if nothing in my ministry or my life was moving. I began to ask the Lord what I was doing wrong and why I couldn't establish a platform to broadcast what he called me to do.

I started reading more into Abraham's story and realized that there was something bigger than who and where I was, that required me to leave the place I called home my entire life. This was a calling that was so potent and unique that I had to depart from the familiar while trusting and being obedient to God. It's safe to say that I acknowledged that it was time to go! Believe it or not, this may be your story. Maybe the Lord has promised you something extraordinary like Abraham, but you missed the first command of the doctrine, which is "It's Time To Go"!

Abram's response to God's call is a shining example of faith and obedience. Without hesitation, he journeyed to the land of Canaan, demonstrating steady faith in the Lord's promises. He built an altar and worshiped God, recognizing His sovereignty and acknowledging His goodness.

As we reflect on Abram's faith, let us examine our own lives. Are we willing to trust God wholeheartedly? Are we ready to step out in faith, even when the path ahead seems uncertain? Are we ready to acknowledge that maybe it's time to go?

Just as God called Abram, He calls each one of us to a unique purpose, and it is in our response to this call that we find fulfillment and blessings beyond measure.

May the story of Abram's faith inspire us to trust in God's promises, to step out in obedience, and to worship Him with all our hearts.

Prayer:

Heavenly Father,

We bow before You with hearts open to receive the message of "It's Time To Go." As we delve into the story of Abram, who became Abraham, we recognize the profound lesson on faith and obedience that it holds.

Lord, we acknowledge that when You call us, it often requires us to step out of our comfort zones and trust in Your guidance. Just as Abram left everything familiar to fulfill Your supernatural calling, we pray for the courage and faith to follow Your lead in our lives.

Genesis 12 reveals Your command to Abram to go to an unknown land, leaving behind his country, family, and father's household. We are reminded of the promises You made to Abram, assuring him of blessings and making him a father of many nations.

As Abram transitioned to become Abraham, we see the significance of the name change representing a shift in focus and destiny. The wisdom gained is that the Abraham of the new could not emerge if he clung to the old as Abram. We pray for the discernment to recognize when it's time to go, to let go of the familiar, and step into the destiny You have written for us.

Lord, like the personal journey shared, where the call to leave Dallas was answered with obedience, we pray for clarity in understanding Your unique calling on our lives. Help us, Lord, to respond with faith and obedience, acknowledging when it's time to go. In Jesus name we pray, Amen!

The key points of this message entitled "It's Time To Go," are as follows:

1. **The Lesson of Leaving the Familiar**: The act of leaving behind the familiar teaches us a valuable lesson in regard to faith. It reminds us that when God calls us to do a certain thing, he often requires us to step out of our comfort zones and trust in his guidance.
2. **Abram's Obedience and Faith**: The message explores the story of Abram (later called Abraham) in the book of Genesis. Abram demonstrated trust and obedience by leaving behind his homeland, family, and everything he knew to fulfill God's supernatural calling.
3. **Change of Name**: The change from "Abram" to "Abraham" symbolizes a shift in focus, from a personal legacy to becoming a vessel through which God's redemptive plan for humanity would be realized. This change in name represents a promise of many descendants and powerful nations.
4. **Personal Connection**: The author of the message shares their personal experience of feeling a calling to ministry and realizing that they needed to leave behind their familiar surroundings to fulfill that calling. This experience is related to Abram's journey.

5. **Faith and Obedience**: The message emphasizes the importance of faith and obedience in responding to God's call, just as Abram did. It encourages readers to trust in God's promises, step out in faith even when the path is uncertain, and acknowledge when it's time to go to fulfill their purpose.

6. **Prayer**: The message concludes with a prayer thanking God and asking for guidance for those who are meant to hear this message, emphasizing the importance of acknowledging when it's time to go and live in purpose on purpose.

Overall, this message centers around the themes of faith, obedience, and responding to God's call, using the story of Abram/Abraham as a central example. It encourages readers to reflect on their own journeys and their willingness to trust and obey.

It's Time To Serve

Serving others with humility and selflessness is a key aspect of being a great leader. By putting the needs of others before our own and using our God-given abilities to benefit, uplift, and inspire, we can be effective and create a positive impact in their lives.

What I've learned is that life has nothing to do with you, but everything to do with those around you. Many people have graced me with the honorable title of a leader, and what I've learned through observing Jesus's time here on Earth is that the true essence of leadership is servitude.

I'd like to take a few moments to walk in the point of view of Jesus Christ and see what the true meaning of service entails.

This message is entitled "It's Time To Serve".

Jesus came not to be served but to serve (Mark 10:45). He walked among us, healing the sick, comforting the brokenhearted, and reaching out to those in need. His life was a living testimony of selflessness and sacrificial love. As His followers, we are called to emulate His example, reflecting His light in the world.

In Luke 10:25-37 (The Parable of the Good Samaritan), Jesus tells a story of a man who was robbed, beaten, and left for dead on the side of the road. A priest and a Levite, both considered prominent religious leaders during that time, passed by and did nothing to help the man. However, a Samaritan passed by, saw the wounded man, and showed compassion, caring for him. Without hesitation, he bandaged his wounds, took him to an inn, and paid for his care. Jesus used this parable to show the importance of serving others by loving our neighbors as ourselves and giving endless mercy for one another.

During the Last Supper, Jesus took on the role of a servant and washed the feet of His disciples. This act of humility shocked and confused the disciples because foot washing was typically performed by the lowest servant. The fact that the Son of Man (the Lamb of God) could get down on his knees and submit himself to serving his disciples in the lowest form reflects that you are never too good or too high to serve!

Jesus explained that He was setting an example for them to follow, teaching them that true leadership comes from serving others. He instructs them that they should do for others what he has done for them.

Friends, serving others is not merely an obligation; it is a source of immense joy and fulfillment. In Acts 20:35, Jesus Himself said, "It is more blessed to give than to receive." When we serve selflessly, we experience the joy of making a positive impact in someone's life.

Believe it or not, our acts of service have a ripple effect. They not only bless those we serve but also inspire others to join in acts of kindness and compassion. As stated in Galatians 6:9, "Let us not become weary in doing good, for at the proper time, we will reap a harvest if we do not give up." Our consistent acts of service plant seeds of hope, love, and transformation in the lives of others.

In Matthew 25:40, Jesus assures us that whatever we do for the least of our brothers and sisters, we do for Him. This divine promise demonstrates that our service to others is an opportunity to encounter the living God in a profound way. It is an expression of our faith and a response to the love and grace we have received from our Heavenly Father.

You know, serving doesn't always have to be a big ordeal. You can actually serve right in the comfort of your own home. I personally believe that the smallest act of serving makes the largest difference. For all the husbands out there (if you're not doing so already), I challenge you to open the car door for your wife or maybe once a week stop by the store on the way home and gather her a bouquet of beautiful flowers with a touching card just because.

For the wives of the world, maybe once a month or every other month, you be the one to book the reservation and treat your husband to dinner at a nice restaurant.

With these examples, not only are you putting others before yourself and serving, but you are also staying connected and building camaraderie with one another.

Friends, sometimes, we may encounter barriers that hinder our willingness to serve. These barriers can include pride, selfishness, busyness, or even fear of the unknown. But just as we witnessed through Jesus, It is more blessed to give than to receive, and that we should do for others what he has done for us. And that is... serve!

Let us never underestimate the impact we can make through acts of service, both big and small. May we remember the words of Galatians 5:13, "Serve one another humbly in love." By following the example of Jesus, we can become instruments of God's love and bring hope, healing, and transformation to a world in need.

Prayer:

Heavenly Father,

We come before You with hearts open to the message of "It's Time To Serve." Lord, teach us the true essence of leadership, which is servitude, as demonstrated by our Lord Jesus Christ during His time on Earth.

Jesus came not to be served but to serve, walking among us with healing, comfort, and compassion. We reflect on the Parable of the Good Samaritan, where Jesus emphasizes the importance of serving others and showing love and mercy.

During the Last Supper, Jesus humbly washed the feet of His disciples, setting an example of true leadership through service. He instructed His disciples to follow His example, revealing that true greatness comes from serving others.

We acknowledge, Lord, that serving others is not merely an obligation but a source of joy and fulfillment. Help us not to grow weary in doing good, knowing that, at the proper time, we will reap a harvest if we do not give up.

May we be inspired by the words of Jesus, "It is more blessed to give than to receive." Let our acts of service be a blessing to those around us, planting seeds of hope, love, and transformation.

Lord, remove any barriers that hinder our willingness to serve, such as pride, selfishness, busyness, or fear. Grant us the humility to serve one another in love, following the example of our Savior.

We pray for marriages and relationships, that they may be strengthened through acts of service, both big and small. May we, as Your instruments, bring hope, healing, and transformation to a world in need. In Jesus name we pray, Amen!

The key points of this message entitled "It's Time To Serve" are as follows:

1. **Leadership through Service:** Serving others with humility and selflessness is highlighted as a crucial aspect of being a great leader. The emphasis is on putting the needs of others before our own and using God-given abilities to benefit, uplift, and inspire.
2. **Jesus as the Exemplar of Service:** The message emphasizes that Jesus came not to be served but to serve, using Mark 10:45 as a reference. Jesus' life is presented as a testimony of selflessness and sacrificial love, and followers are called to emulate His example.

3. **The Good Samaritan Parable:** The story of the Good Samaritan (Luke 10:25-37) is used to illustrate the importance of serving others with love and mercy. It underlines the idea of loving neighbors as oneself and the impact of compassionate actions.

4. **Humility in Service:** The message recounts the episode of Jesus washing the disciples' feet during the Last Supper, highlighting the humility of true leadership. The disciples' initial confusion underscores the idea that no one is too good or too high to serve.

5. **Joy and Fulfillment in Service:** Serving others is portrayed not just as an obligation but as a source of immense joy and fulfillment. The message quotes Acts 20:35, where Jesus states that it is more blessed to give than to receive.

6. **Ripple Effect of Acts of Service:** Acts of service are described as having a ripple effect, blessing not only those served but inspiring others to engage in kindness and compassion. Galatians 6:9 is cited to emphasize the importance of persistence in doing good.

7. **Encounter with God Through Service:** Matthew 25:40 is referenced to convey that serving others is an opportunity to encounter the living God. Service is seen as an expression of faith and a response to the love and grace received from God.

8. **Everyday Acts of Service:** The message encourages small acts of service in everyday life, such as opening doors or surprising loved ones with gestures of kindness. Examples are provided for husbands and wives to serve each other, fostering connection and camaraderie.

9. **Overcoming Barriers to Service:** Barriers to serving others, such as pride, selfishness, busyness, or fear, are acknowledged and should be overcome. The message encourages following Jesus' example of giving and serving.

10. **Impact of Acts of Service:** Acts of service, regardless of size, are presented as having a lasting impact on individuals and communities. The message concludes with a call to never underestimate the impact of service.

11. **Prayer and Gratitude:** The message ends with a prayer expressing gratitude for the message and a request for blessings on those who have received it. The prayer acknowledges the grace received from God and asks for blessings on the audience.

Overall, this message strongly emphasizes the transformative power of humble service, using biblical examples and practical suggestions to encourage a mindset of selfless giving and kindness.

Joy Is Enough

In a world full of possibilities, endless opportunities, and free will, we encounter this seven-letter word called "choices." So why not choose to have something substantial?

This message is entitled "Joy Is Enough."

You don't want happiness; you want joy! Did you know that being happy is actually temporary? As a matter of fact, happiness is based on your happenings, but real joy comes from the Lord. You are happy when your funds are low, and that Good Friday hits, and you get paid, but when that next Friday comes around and those funds are gone, that temporary feeling starts to fade. You are happy when the weekend arrives, enabling you to sleep in and enjoy quality time with friends and family, but when Monday morning arrives, that temporary feeling starts to disappear, and you're already looking forward to the next weekend.

Here's my favorite example... You are a single individual feeling alone and figure that void will only be filled once you find love. So, you go out, find your partner, and then get married thinking that all your problems will go away. Now you're four months into marriage, and you don't like when their leg touches yours when you're sleeping in bed, and you have a problem with the way they eat and dress. So, that temporary feeling starts to go away, and you're not even a year in, already asking for a divorce. Why? Because happiness is based on your happenings.

Now let me tell you about this three-letter word known as joy! Joy is when all hell is breaking loose, but you still have peace. Joy is when you're alone, but your own company is satisfactory to you. Joy is when people are talking down on you, but you're not worried about what they

75

say because God says something totally different about you. Joy is being broke but still having a smile on your face and making use of what you have, knowing that what you have is all you need.

Joy is sustainable, sufficient, adequate, permanent, divine, the reason why you get up in the morning, your source of love because God is love, and joy is enough! I just love what Isaiah 55:12 says; it reads: "You will indeed go out with joy and be peacefully guided; the mountains and the hills will break into singing before you, and all the trees of the fields will clap their hands."

Here's a quote by Henry J.M Nowin... "Joy does not simply happen to us; we have to choose joy and keep choosing it every single day." Friends, stop thinking that joy is external. You don't need all the designer bags, foreign cars, and fancy dresses and suits to fill that empty hole inside of you. Yeah, those things are nice to have, and they make us look great and feel great, but those things are not substantial. The only permanent source known to man is the joy that comes from knowing your creator! And He who does a great work in you shall perform it until the day of Jesus Christ!

I want to encourage you to stop asking for happiness and find joy! The only way to find joy is through Christ; otherwise, your circumstances will determine your reality. So, remember, happiness is based on your happenings, but real joy... true joy... authentic joy comes from the Lord!

Prayer:

Heavenly Father,

As we bow before you today, we thank you for the profound truth shared in this message, "Joy Is Enough." In a world that often confuses happiness with joy, we seek your wisdom and understanding.

Lord, help us to recognize that true joy is not based on external circumstances but is a gift from You. We choose joy, knowing that it is sustainable, sufficient, and divine. It is not fleeting like happiness but a permanent source that comes from knowing You, our Creator.

Thank you for the reminder from Isaiah 55:12 that we can go out with joy and be peacefully guided by Your hand. In the midst of challenges, help us to experience the joy that surpasses understanding, a joy that remains despite the ups and downs of life.

We acknowledge that joy is a choice, and we choose to find joy in You every single day. Your love, peace, and promises bring a joy that transcends our circumstances.

Lord, free us from the misconception that material possessions and external achievements can fill the void inside us. May we understand that true, authentic joy comes from a relationship with You. We surrender our desire for mere happiness and instead seek the enduring joy that only You can provide.

May this message resonate with our hearts, reminding us to choose joy daily. In moments of difficulty, may we lean on Your everlasting joy to sustain us. Thank you for being our source of joy, love, and peace. In Jesus name we pray, Amen!

The key points of this message entitled "Joy Is Enough" are as follows:

- **Choosing Joy Over Happiness**: The message emphasizes the distinction between happiness and joy. Happiness is described as temporary and dependent on external circumstances or "happenings," while joy is portrayed as something deeper and more lasting, stemming from a divine source.
- **Happiness vs. Joy**: The message provides examples of how happiness can be fleeting, such as the excitement of payday, weekends, or new relationships, which can diminish over time when faced with everyday challenges.
- **Characteristics of Joy**: Joy is presented as something sustainable, permanent, divine, and self-sufficient. It is highlighted as the

reason for peace, contentment, and a positive outlook, even in the midst of difficult circumstances.

- **Biblical Reference**: Isaiah 55:12 is quoted to support the concept of joy. The verse speaks of going out with joy, being peacefully guided, and the natural world rejoicing along with the individual experiencing joy.
- **Choosing Joy Daily**: The message quotes Henry J.M Nowin, stating that joy is a choice that must be made daily. It encourages readers to actively choose joy in their lives, despite external circumstances.
- **Internal Source of Joy**: The message suggests that joy is not found in external possessions, such as designer bags, cars, or fancy attire. Instead, it asserts that true joy is found within and is rooted in one's relationship with their Creator.
- **The Role of Christ**: The essence is that authentic joy comes from knowing Christ. It is presented as an internal, spiritual source of contentment that transcends external circumstances. The devotional encourages readers to seek joy through their faith in Christ.
- **Prayer**: The message concludes with a prayer, thanking God for joy and asking for His guidance in finding and choosing joy. It also expresses a desire for readers not to seek temporary external sources of happiness, like pornography or drugs, but to find lasting joy in their relationship with God.

Overall, this message inspires readers to seek joy within themselves, rooted in their faith, rather than relying on external circumstances or possessions for happiness. It emphasizes that joy is a choice and an internal state of being that can be sustained even in challenging times.

Keep The Vision

I personally am a huge advocate for vision. Vision is the driving factor in why I do what I do. You should never live life without being able to see your destination because, in retrospect, if you cannot see, where exactly are you going? It's safe to say that if the way is clear, and the path is smooth, then it is very easy to ideate the vision.

Now, what if the way isn't clear and the path isn't smooth? What if things don't go as planned, and somewhere in the process gets delayed? What if you lose someone or something that you thought would be there in the end? What if you find yourself in a season in which it gets very difficult to envision the actual vision?

This message is entitled "Keep The Vision"!

Since August of 2021, I've always had a vision board in my bedroom. As the months go by, my vision board changes based on the completion of what was on it during that time frame. I place my vision board strategically in alignment with my bed on the opposite wall; therefore, when I wake up in the morning, it is the first thing I see to remind me of my "Why."

As I stated earlier, if you cannot see, where exactly are you going? We must remember that God has a purpose for our lives, and sometimes we go down paths and invest time, money, and effort into things that weren't even meant for us in the first place.

A person from a biblical context that can relate to such is Habakkuk. Habakkuk was greatly concerned about the spiritual deterioration of God's people and begged God for assistance as he observed the blazing worldwide scene and the wickedness, suffering, and injustice that were consuming the kingdom of Judah.

In the Lord's second answer to Habakkuk in chapter 2, He said to him… "Write down this vision. Clearly inscribe it on tablets so one may easily read it. For the vision is yet for the appointed time; it testifies about the end and will not lie. Though it delays, wait for it, since it will certainly come and not be late."

The part of this scripture that I love the most is the end of verse 3 when it says, "Though it delays, wait for it, since it will certainly come and not be late." There he learned that God was not unconcerned with His people's suffering, but he also realized that the Lord had set aside a glorious time when He would deliver His people from their sins and their adversaries and wipe away every tear from their eyes.

Things were going to get worse before they got better in Habakkuk's day, so he was urged to hold on to his faith and put his trust in the Lord, who is dependable to save His people and stay true to His Word. Believe it or not, that same principle is still in effect today.

Friends, anything that God has for you, you must be prepared for. It is in the preparation phase where He's building you, molding you, strengthening you, giving you courage, and giving you vision. Some of us feel that if God is not answering us right away or taking us out of situations immediately, it means that He's forgotten about us, or that our reservations to our purpose have been canceled.

It's so hard to keep maintaining not knowing how long you have to wait or what's on the other side, but I want to encourage you to throw your faith on your back and continue to move forward. And that's my prayer for you today… that you keep the vision. Things may look chaotic now, but keep the vision. Your timeframe and God's timeframe may not align, but keep the vision. People may tell you that there's no power coming from God's purpose for your life, but keep the vision. And just as the Lord said to Habakkuk, "Though it delays, wait for it, since it will certainly come and not be late."

Prayer:

Heavenly Father,

As we come before you in prayer, we thank you for the message that encourages us to "Keep The Vision." Lord, you are the ultimate source of purpose and vision in our lives, and we acknowledge that our steps are guided by your divine plan.

In moments when the path becomes unclear and obstacles arise, help us, O Lord, to hold on to the vision you've placed within our hearts. Just as Habakkuk inscribed the vision on tablets, may we engrave your purpose for our lives deeply in our hearts and minds.

Lord, we understand that delays do not mean denials in your perfect timing. Grant us the patience to wait for your appointed time, knowing that your promises are true and will come to fruition. Strengthen our faith during the seasons of waiting, and may we find solace in the assurance that you are faithful to your Word.

We pray for those who may be facing challenges, feeling discouraged, or struggling to envision the path ahead. Lord, ignite within them a renewed sense of purpose and vision. Let your Spirit remind them that you are working in the midst of delays, preparing, molding, and building them for the fulfillment of your divine plan.

May this message resonate in our hearts, inspiring us to keep the vision alive. Help us to move forward with faith, even when circumstances seem chaotic. In Jesus name we pray, Amen!

The key points of this message entitled "Keep The Vision" are as follows:

1. **The Importance of Vision**: The author emphasizes the importance of having a vision in life, as it serves as a driving force and a guiding light for one's actions and decisions. The

idea is that without a vision, it's challenging to know where you're going.

2. **Challenges to Maintaining the Vision**: The message raises questions about what happens when the path isn't clear, things don't go as planned, or when it becomes difficult to envision the original vision.

3. **Biblical Context - Habakkuk**: The message introduces the biblical figure Habakkuk, who was concerned about the spiritual deterioration of God's people and sought God's guidance in the midst of a challenging and unjust world.

4. **God's Response to Habakkuk**: In God's response to Habakkuk in chapter 2, God instructs him to write down the vision clearly and assures him that it has an appointed time. The verse highlights the importance of patience and waiting for the fulfillment of the vision.

5. **"Though it Delays, wait for it"**: The message emphasizes the message from the end of verse 3 in Habakkuk 2, which encourages waiting for the vision even if it seems delayed. It suggests that God's timing is different from human expectations but is always dependable.

6. **The Preparation Phase**: The author points out that during the waiting period, God is preparing, molding, strengthening, and building individuals for the realization of their vision. It's a time of growth and development.

7. **Maintaining Faith**: The message encourages readers to maintain their faith even when they don't see immediate answers to their prayers or changes in their circumstances. It suggests that God has not forgotten them, and His purpose for their lives remains intact.

8. **Keep the Vision**: The central idea is to keep the vision alive, even when faced with chaos, delays, or discouragement. It encourages readers to trust in God's timing and faithfulness.

Prayer: The message concludes with a prayer asking for strength, encouragement, and motivation for those who read it, so they may keep their vision and maintain their faith despite challenges.

Overall, this message underscores the importance of having a vision in life and the need to hold onto it even when circumstances are challenging or uncertain. It draws from the biblical example of Habakkuk to illustrate the concept of waiting for God's appointed time and remaining steadfast in faith.

Living In Expectation

Expectation is the key determinant of all faith! Yeah, I know you pray, and I know you ask God to move things around in your life, but in return, are you expecting it?

Are you walking around with the clarity that God is going to deliver on His promise?

Believe it or not, the Lord wants to do miraculous things in you and through you, but He first wants to see if you are living in the expectation of what He can do!

He wants to see what your faith is all about!

This message is entitled "Living In Expectation"!

Psalms 5 reads, "Listen to my words, Lord, consider my lament. Hear my cry for help, my King and my God, for to you, I pray. In the morning, Lord, you will hear my voice; in the morning I lay my request before you and wait expectantly."

In this text, David promises the Lord that he will pray early in the morning. David is teaching us that it is eagerly important to pray, but it is also equally as important to look and listen for God's answer to your prayers. That's why in the Psalms David utters "I will watch and pray".

You see when we pray, we are required to exhibit positive expectation. Jesus said in Matthew 7, "Ask and it will be given to you; seek and you will find; knock and the door will be opened to you. For everyone who

85

asks receives; the one who seeks finds, and to the one who knocks, the door will be opened."

In 1 Kings, Elijah sent his servant to go and check on the weather as he prayed for rain to fall. He only anticipated rain. Elijah then declared that heavy rain was about to start falling when the servant reported there was something resembling a small hand in the cloud. It's safe to say that Elijah was living in expectation!

The woman with the issue of blood spoke "if I may but touch the hem of his garment, I shall be made whole. She was living in the expectation that Jesus had the power and authority to heal her if she came close enough to touch his clothing. Jesus then told her "Because of your faith, you have been healed".

Blind Bartimaeus kept shouting towards Jesus when others told him to stop, in the expectation that the Lord could make his blind eyes see. Jesus called him over and said "You may go. Your eyes are healed because of your faith."

At the gate called Beautiful, a man from birth who couldn't walk was being carried to the temple. When he saw Peter and John about to enter, he asked them for money. Peter and John looked straight at him. The man gave them his attention, expecting to get something from them. Peter then uttered "In the mighty name of Jesus, Walk! And so, he did.

Simply said, every one of us who practices faith must live each day with hope in our hearts. When we put our trust in the Lord, we should live in the mentality that He will shower us with blessings every single day.

Living in expectation makes you think positively. You gain a cheerful outlook on things. Living in expectation demonstrates our faith in God, our reliance on His word, and our assurance of His promises. Living with expectations serves as a reminder of our obligations to one another. If we want good things to happen to us, we should endeavor to conduct good deeds that are also expected of us.

We anticipate Christ's second coming to judge the earth. Knowing that everything will be exposed before the judgment seat at some point keeps us fully aware of how we live.

Friends, I'll be one to tell you that living in expectation isn't always an easy task. It's tough to expect in confusion, uncertainty, pain, and turmoil, when you can't find a job, when there's not any money coming in, when food becomes scarce, when love is lost, when you keep getting NO for an answer, when doctors can't do anything else, or when what you've been waiting for gets delayed.

But I'll also tell you that Expectation is the key determinant of all faith!

When you expect nothing to happen, nothing happens. When you expect miracles, miraculous things take place!

The Bible says, "For just as the body without the spirit is dead, so also faith without works is dead". It's imperative that you understand that the work of your faith is your expectation! When in the season of expecting, you are making room for something. This means you are enacting your faith by being in a position for the blessing that you are expecting.

We noticed earlier in our examples from our brothers and sisters in the Bible that none of them prayed and just stayed put. They were all on the move and making sure that when the Lord came their way, they were in a position to receive what they were expecting.

Why? Because Expectation is the key determinant of all faith!

So, my questions for you today are...

Are you living in expectation? Are you in a position to receive what you're expecting? If not…. Then let's start today!

Prayer:

Heavenly Father,

We come before you with hearts filled with gratitude for your love and the promise of your blessings. Lord, we thank you for the powerful message of "Living In Expectation." In a world filled with uncertainties, help us to anchor our faith in the expectation of what you can do in our lives.

As we lift our prayers and requests before you, may we not only ask but also wait expectantly, just as David did in Psalms 5. Teach us to pray with the understanding that you hear our cries, and in the morning, we will wait expectantly for your response.

Your Word tells us that if we ask, seek, and knock, we will receive, find, and have doors opened for us. Help us to walk with clarity, fully expecting your deliverance and the fulfillment of your promises in our lives. Strengthen our faith, Lord, that we may live each day with hope in our hearts, anticipating the shower of your blessings.

Just like the examples of faith from the Bible—Elijah, the woman with the issue of blood, Blind Bartimaeus, and the man at the gate called Beautiful—may we live in expectation, believing in your power to bring about miraculous things. In Jesus name we pray, Amen!

The key points of this message entitled "Living In Expectation" are as follows:

1. **Expectation and Faith**: The message begins by emphasizing the importance of expectation in determining one's faith. It suggests that while people may pray and seek God's intervention, true faith involves expecting God to fulfill His promises.

2. **Prayer and Positive Expectation**: The text from Psalms 5 is cited as an example where David not only prayed but also waited expectantly for God's response. It highlights the idea that prayer should be accompanied by positive expectations.

3. **Biblical Examples**: The message draws attention to several biblical examples where individuals demonstrated expectation in their faith:
   - Elijah expected rain and declared it before it happened.
   - The woman with the issue of blood expected healing by touching Jesus' garment and her faith was rewarded.
   - Blind Bartimaeus expected Jesus to restore his sight and called out persistently.
   - The beggar at the gate called Beautiful expected to receive something from Peter and John and was healed.

4. **Living in Expectation**: The core message is that living in expectation means living each day with hope, a cheerful outlook, and the assurance of God's promises. It encourages a mindset of expecting blessings and living with faith in God's provision.

5. **The Works of Faith**: The message links expectation to the "works of faith" mentioned in the Bible, highlighting that being in a state of expectation positions one to receive blessings and answers to prayer.

6. **Challenges and Expectations**: It acknowledges that living in expectation can be challenging, especially in difficult circumstances. However, it reiterates the idea that expectation is a key factor in the manifestation of faith and miracles.

7. **Final Questions**: The message concludes by asking the reader if they are living in expectation and if they are in a position to receive what they are expecting. It emphasizes the importance of acting and being prepared to receive God's blessings.

Overall, this message motivates believers to cultivate positive expectations in their faith and trust that God will fulfill His promises when they pray and remain in a state of hopeful anticipation. It underscores the connection between expectation and faith as a dynamic force in the life of a believer.

Look In Your Hand

———

This message is entitled "Look In Your Hand."

A couple of weeks ago, I saw this headline about a man who suddenly decided to rob his local bank. It really caught my attention, so I wanted to dive deeper into the story. Obviously, his reasoning for robbing the bank was to get more money.

The man went into the bank and held one of the bank tellers at gunpoint, demanding her to open the safe. After a brief confrontation, he ended up taking $9,000.

As I looked at the police report, it said that the man was arrested within 20 minutes of the attempted robbery.

As the investigation went on, they performed a very complex analysis of the gun used in the robbery. The name of the gun is a Colt Python Stalker (from the late 1980s), which is listed today at around $18,000.

So, that means that the value of the gun is worth nearly double the amount of money that the man had stolen from the bank.

I took a minute and thought to myself, MAN… If this dude just realized what he had in his hand, he'd come to the understanding that he already had what he wanted.

And friends, just like this man, sometimes we tend to have the ill-advised, fleshly desire to go after something in response to God's silence of our asking and fail to realize that maybe if we'd just look in our hands, we'd obtain a comprehensive understanding that what we long for we already possess because He has given it to us.

I love what 2 Peter 1:3 says… it reads, "His divine power has given us everything required for life and godliness through the knowledge of him who called us by his own glory and goodness."

This verse shows that everything we require for survival has already been provided for us by God. We are equipped to handle everything. We already have access to all the possibilities, knowledge, and connections thanks to knowing Him.

Now, also take note that sometimes it won't be in black and white.

There's a segment by Bishop TD Jakes, and he says God doesn't make furniture; he makes trees.

What he's trying to articulate is that don't think that the thing you're looking for is going to come gift-wrapped and handed to you.

You see, before the furniture is furniture, they have to cut down the tree, and shred it, and carve it, and shape it into that chair, or that table, or that couch.

Sometimes you have to dig through your closet, shuffle through things under your bed, or scavenge through that old storage of yours because, believe it or not, what you have is all you need.

And so, my challenge for you is to find your tree and use that tree to make your furniture. Whether that be in your finances, in your relationships, at the job site, or even in your mental and physical health. Because what you have is all you need.

Prayer:

Heavenly Father,

We come before you with gratitude for the reminder that everything we need for life and godliness has already been provided by your divine power. Your Word declares that we have access to all the possibilities, knowledge, and connections through the knowledge of you.

Lord, help us to recognize the treasures in our hands. Sometimes, in our pursuit of desires, we may overlook the abundant blessings already present in our lives. Open our eyes to see the value of what we already possess and to appreciate the gifts you have bestowed upon us.

In moments of longing and unanswered prayers, may we pause and reflect on the truth that you have given us everything required for life and godliness. Strengthen our faith to trust in your divine provision and guidance. As Bishop TD Jakes wisely noted, help us understand that sometimes the things we seek may not come gift-wrapped, but they are present in the raw materials you've provided.

Lord, grant us the wisdom to discern and utilize the resources, talents, and opportunities already in our possession. May we find our "trees" and, with your guidance, transform them into the furniture of our lives—whether in our finances, relationships, work, or health.

We thank you, Lord, for the assurance that what we have is all we need. Instill in us a spirit of contentment and gratitude for your abundant blessings. In times of uncertainty, help us trust in your plan and recognize the beauty in the gifts that may not always be apparent at first glance. In Jesus name we pray, Amen!

The key points of this message entitled "Look In Your Hand" are as follows:

1. **Introduction:** The message begins with a story about a man who attempted to rob a bank to get more money but didn't realize the value of the gun he was using.
2. **Missed Opportunity:** The man robs the bank for $9,000 but doesn't realize that the gun he used, a Colt Python Stalker from the late 1980s, is worth nearly double that amount.
3. **Spiritual Message:** The message draws a parallel between the man's situation and how people sometimes seek external solutions or desires when they already possess what they need. It emphasizes the importance of recognizing what you already have.
4. **Scriptural Reference:** The message quotes 2 Peter 1:3, which highlights that God's divine power has provided everything required for life and godliness through the knowledge of Him.
5. **Not Always Black and White:** It mentions that what you need might not always be obvious or readily apparent. Sometimes, you must search, dig, or be resourceful to discover what you already possess.
6. **Challenge:** The message challenges readers to find their "tree" (the source) and use it to make their "furniture" (solutions or blessings) in various aspects of life, such as finances, relationships, work, and health.
7. **Prayer:** The devotional concludes with a prayer, thanking God for the message and asking that readers utilize it to acknowledge that they already have what they need.

Overall, this message moves readers to recognize the blessings and resources they already have in their lives, rather than constantly seeking external solutions, and to be resourceful in utilizing what they possess to achieve their goals.

Love Guided Actions

In this moment,, I want to touch base on one of the many sound doctrines taught by the apostle Paul later in the New Testament in 1 Timothy.

This message is entitled "Love-Guided Actions."

So, Paul, who is an Apostle of Christ, is writing a letter to Timothy, who he calls his true son in the faith. In the letter, Paul instructs Timothy to go to the city of Ephesus and stop those who are teaching false doctrines and worshiping myths.

1 Timothy 1 reads this way:

"Paul, an apostle of Christ Jesus by the command of God our Savior and of Christ Jesus our hope: To Timothy, my true son in the faith. Grace, mercy, and peace from God the Father and Christ Jesus our Lord.

As I urged you when I went to Macedonia, remain in Ephesus so that you may instruct certain people not to teach false doctrine or to pay attention to myths and endless genealogies.

These promote empty speculations rather than God's plan, which operates by faith. Now the goal of our instruction is love that comes from a pure heart, a good conscience, and a sincere faith. Some have departed from these and turned aside to fruitless discussion."

Now, Timothy had a crucial task ahead of him in doing this. The crowd that Timothy was assigned to was already known for teaching against God's plan, which was considered unholy and irrelevant. The crowd could consist of those who kill their fathers and mothers, the sexually immoral, the murderers, slave traders, liars, homosexuals, and perjurers.

Paul then takes a moment to stop and testify about the everlasting love that Jesus Christ brings. Prior to Paul's ministry, he used to be a blasphemer, a Christian killer, and a very arrogant man but received mercy when he acted out of ignorance and disbelief, and the grace of the Lord's love overflowed, and he became faithful.

I want to go back to verse 5 here. It says, "The goal of our instruction is love."

Through all this that is happening, the Apostle Paul is demonstrating that although what they are doing is wrong, this call to action is coming from the heart, which is a place of love, not a place of hate.

The way people will conceive the words that you utter is strictly dependent on where they're coming from!

I remember as a child when I'd do something wrong, my mom would discipline me! She'd always take something away, yell at me, or tell me I can't go outside for the day. I used to always think to myself, "Ugh, she's just a mean lady" or "She dislikes me." But after she disciplined me, she'd always follow up and tell me, "Jonathyn, I do what I do because I love you."

And friends, it's the same concept here. After Paul urges Timothy to go and correct the people in the city of Ephesus for their wrongdoings, he then reminds them of the same thing my mom reminded me all those years ago: the goal of this command is just simply love!

I want to encourage you for the next time you are talking with someone or correcting and are trying to get a point across, remind them that "it's all out of love."

Always remember, once upon a time, the person being corrected was you, and it was the Lord's overflow of abundant grace, mercy, and love that forgave you and considered you faithful.

Prayer:

Gracious Father,

We come before you with gratitude for the wisdom shared through the Apostle Paul's teachings in 1 Timothy. Thank you for the guidance and insights into the importance of love-guided actions.

Lord, we acknowledge that, like Timothy, we are sometimes called to correct and guide others in the path of righteousness. As we engage in such conversations, help us to do so with hearts filled with love, compassion, and understanding. May our words and actions reflect the genuine concern we have for those we are addressing.

Your Word reminds us that the goal of our instruction is love—a love that emanates from a pure heart, a good conscience, and a sincere faith. Teach us, Lord, to approach correction and guidance with humility, recognizing that we too have received your abundant grace, mercy, and love.

Just as Paul testified to the transformative power of your love in his life, may our interactions be guided by the same love that overflowed in our own salvation. Help us to convey to others that our desire to guide and correct is rooted in love, just as a parent disciplines a child out of love.

Grant us the ability to see beyond the actions and behaviors to the hearts of those we interact with. May our efforts to correct be infused with empathy and a genuine desire for the well-being of those we seek to guide. In Jesus name I pray, Amen!

The key points of this message entitled "Love Guided Actions" are as follows:

1. **Introduction:** The message begins by introducing the concept of "Love Guided Actions" and mentions that it is inspired by the teachings of the apostle Paul in the New Testament, particularly in 1 Timothy.

2. **Paul's Letter to Timothy:** The message provides background information on Paul, who is writing a letter to Timothy, referring to him as his true son in the faith. In the letter, Paul instructs Timothy to address and correct false teachings and myths being promoted in the city of Ephesus.

3. **Scriptural Reference (1 Timothy 1):** The message quotes 1 Timothy 1, emphasizing the importance of instructing certain individuals not to teach false doctrines or focus on myths and genealogies. It mentions that these teachings promote empty speculations rather than God's plan, which operates through faith.

4. **The Goal of Instruction Is Love:** The message highlights verse 5 of 1 Timothy 1, which states, "The goal of our instruction is love that comes from a pure heart, a good conscience, and a sincere faith." It emphasizes that despite the need for correction, the actions are driven by love, not hate.

5. **Personal Connection:** The author shares a personal story about how, as a child, their mother disciplined them out of love, even though it may have seemed harsh at the time. This serves as an example of how correction and instruction can be motivated by love.

6. **Reminder to Express Love:** The message encourages readers to remember that when correcting or instructing others, it's essential to communicate that it's all done out of love. This can help the person being corrected understand the intentions behind the actions.

7. **Final Prayer:** The message concludes with a prayer, thanking the Lord for the day and asking for guidance in using the message as a guide to be better servants of God's kingdom.

Overall, this message emphasizes the importance of correcting and instructing others with love as the guiding motive, just as Paul instructed Timothy to address false teachings out of love for the faith and the people involved.

Perfect Timing

The Book of Acts is written by St. Luke, who is also the 3rd representative of Jesus in the Gospels earlier in the New Testament.

Here in this timeframe, Jesus has just been resurrected from the dead. Amongst Jesus are his twelve disciples, who are very excited. However, Jesus is telling them to wait and stay here in Jerusalem for the Father's promise.

Before his ascension into heaven, Jesus was informing the apostles by saying this to stay focused on spreading the gospel rather than getting caught up in the fulfillment of prophecies. He will give them the authority to do so. However, He wanted them to focus on the current task.

So, let's go to the text! Starting in Chapter 1, verse 4… (4) And being assembled together with them, He commanded them not to depart from Jerusalem, but to wait for the Promise of the Father, "which," He said, "you have heard from Me.

(5) For John truly baptized with water, but you shall be baptized with the Holy Spirit not many days from now."

(6) Therefore, when they had come together, they asked Him, saying, "Lord, will You at this time restore the kingdom to Israel?"

(7) And He said to them, "It is not for you to know times or seasons which the Father has put in His own authority.

(8) But you shall receive power when the Holy Spirit has come upon you, and you shall be witnesses to Me in Jerusalem, and in all Judea and Samaria, and to the end of the earth.

I want to put emphasis on verses 7 and 8 of this text! They read…

(7) And He said to them, "It is not for you to know times or seasons which the Father has put in His own authority.

(8) But you shall receive power when the Holy Spirit has come upon you, and you shall be witnesses to Me in Jerusalem, and in all Judea and Samaria, and to the end of the earth.

This message is entitled "Perfect Timing."

In many scenarios, we find it very difficult to work on a task at hand while at the same time waiting on something. Many of you know what it's like to live in the excitement or the anxiety of working diligently while waiting patiently.

Working on your job is a great example. Let's say your pay is based on an hourly rate. You've noticed that your weekly hours for the coming weeks have increased drastically, which means you are now in a position for a big increase in your next check. You are now living in the excitement or the anxiety of still working diligently while still waiting patiently.

Believe it or not, waiting and working is the key concept in this text. Though we should be excited and prepared for the (big increase) in Christ's return, we are still to focus on being his witnesses in this world.

Now, before ascending to Heaven, Jesus had issued directives to His chosen disciples through the Holy Spirit. These apostles were the devoted eleven of the twelve disciples who had accompanied and assisted Jesus during His ministry on Earth. The word Apostle means "a person who is sent." It is used in the book of Acts to describe the disciples who were sent by Jesus to tell the world about His death and resurrection.

He explained to them that it was written that Christ would suffer, rise from the dead on the third day, and that repentance for sins would be proclaimed in His name to all peoples, starting in Jerusalem, after He had opened their minds to understand the Scriptures. He says you are witnesses of these things. And behold, I am sending forth the promise of My Father upon you; but you are to stay in the city until you are clothed with power from on high.

We should follow the same guidelines as the apostles even today, nearly 2,000 years later. Since Christ's return could occur at any time, we must surely prepare for it. However, at the same time, we are to be about our father's business by being the salt and light in this world.

We are to work diligently while waiting patiently.

I want to encourage you to maintain a healthy balance between preparing for Christ's return and doing his ministry in the world. That can simply be by:

- Inviting someone to attend church with you, or now is an excellent time to ask them to join you in watching the service online. After that, find out what they thought of the encounter. Talk to them about the message and be prepared to respond to any belief they may have.
- Simply approach someone and ask how you can pray for them. Pay attention to what they need. Ask whether you can pray with them at that time if you think the time is right. Simply let them know that you are thinking of them and that you love them.
- Identify someone you know who needs something. Perhaps a friend of yours lost their job and could use some groceries, or perhaps a new mother could use some beautiful things to pamper herself. Think carefully about what to offer and who to give it to.
- Invite someone to join you in your daily reading, and be prepared to discuss what was read, even if it's just over text. Ask them about their thoughts, their connections, and their takeaways.

- Send some biblical encouragement to someone you know if they are struggling, going through a difficult moment, or just need some love. Spend some time crafting a note that is both hopeful and unique and tell them you are thinking of them in prayer, and that you are always there for them.

And just like Paul said in 1 Corinthians...

"Therefore, my beloved brothers, be steadfast, immovable, always abounding in the work of the Lord, knowing that in the Lord your labor is not in vain."

Although we may not know the day or the hour, we just need to know that the timing is perfect.

Prayer:

Heavenly Father,

We approach Your throne with gratitude for the wisdom shared in the Book of Acts, particularly in the words of Jesus to His disciples. Thank you for reminding us of the importance of perfect timing in our lives.

Lord, as we navigate the complexities of waiting and working, help us find the balance that aligns with Your divine plan. Just as Jesus instructed His disciples to wait for the promise of the Holy Spirit, we too seek patience and trust in Your perfect timing.

In moments of anticipation, may we remain steadfast, understanding that times and seasons are within Your authority. Grant us the discernment to focus on the tasks at hand, diligently working as witnesses to Your love and grace.

As we prepare for the return of Christ, help us not to be consumed by anxiety or distracted by the unknown. Instead, may our attention be devoted to the ministry of spreading the gospel and being the salt and light in this world.

Lord, empower us with Your Holy Spirit, as promised, so that we can be effective witnesses in our communities, reaching out with love and compassion. Guide us in practical ways to share Your message, whether it's inviting others to church, praying for those in need, offering support, or sharing the hope found in Your Word. In Jesus name we pray, Amen!

The key points of this message entitled "Perfect Timing" are as follows:

1. **Biblical Context**: The message starts by setting the context in the Book of Acts, where Jesus has just been resurrected, and he instructs his disciples to wait in Jerusalem for the Father's promise.

2. **Waiting and Working**: It emphasizes the concept of simultaneously waiting and working, drawing parallels to situations in everyday life where one may be excited or anxious while diligently working toward a goal.

3. **Focus on Being Witnesses**: The core message is that while believers should be prepared and excited for Christ's return, they should also focus on being witnesses for Him in the world. The disciples were directed to be witnesses of Jesus and proclaim repentance for sins.

4. **Balancing Preparation and Ministry**: The message encourages believers to find a balance between preparing for Christ's return and actively participating in His ministry. It suggests practical ways to engage in ministry, such as inviting someone to church, praying for others, helping those in need, reading the Bible with someone, and offering biblical encouragement.

5. **1 Corinthians Reference**: The message references 1 Corinthians, highlighting the importance of remaining steadfast and immovable in the work of the Lord, knowing that their labor is not in vain.

6. **The Timing is Perfect**: The message concludes by affirming that even though believers may not know the specific timing of Christ's return, they can trust that it is perfect timing.

Overall, this message underscores the idea that while believers eagerly await Christ's return, they should also actively engage in His work by being witnesses and demonstrating love and compassion in their interactions with others. It encourages a balanced approach to faith that encompasses both preparation and ministry.

Purposeful Pain

There's not a person on this planet that can avoid pain. As a matter of fact, it is an inescapable part of life.

Life can sometimes be unpleasant because we exist in a world torn apart by sin. Almost everyone deals with pain on a daily basis. It can be physical pain, relational pain, mental or emotional pain, financial or social pain, or even spiritual pain, but it hurts no matter what kind of pain it is.

This message is entitled "Purposeful Pain."

Romans 8:28 "For we know that all things work together for the good of those who love God and who are called according to his purpose."

I just love this message that the apostle Paul is writing to the Christian church as he's trying to provide direction, encouragement, and guidance to that community of believers.

This passage assures people who love God and are making every effort to follow his instructions, even if there's bad news, if there are tough circumstances, if there's wickedness towards you, or even evil in your path. God is saying I will utilize these things to ultimately bring about good, both in your life and in the world.

So, there's a show on Netflix I used to watch called 'Sugar Rush". This is a show that consists of baking pastries such as cakes, brownies, pies, and donuts.

The final product of the pastries that were being made really impressed me and inspired me to get into baking. I then went to my local grocery store and bought all the things that were needed to bake a cake. When I started the process, I was in such disbelief that the ingredients I have before me, which by themselves don't taste good at all can make the amazing masterpiece I saw on Sugar Rush.

The first thing I poured into the bowl was flour. Now Flour is a powder that is very gritty and tasteless. The second thing I poured into the bowl was milk, which is a white liquid produced by the mammary glands of mammals. The next thing in the bowl was eggs, which are slimy substances made up almost entirely of calcium carbonate. The fourth thing I poured into the bowl was sugar, which is just gritty, unhealthy, sweet-tasting carbohydrates. The fifth thing to go into the bowl was vegetable oil, which is an odorless, flavorless oil that comes from plants. The last thing to enter the bowl was baking soda, which is just a solution of table salt and carbon dioxide.

Now as I began to observe all the substances in the bowl, I just couldn't fully process how these ingredients which are useless by themselves could make something so rich and tasty. After I finished mixing everything together, I placed it in the oven, and it started to rise into the amazing masterpiece I saw on Sugar Rush.

When this happened, I figured out that it's not the ingredients themselves that made the cake, it is when they all come together in the bowl and become what it was created to be.

What I would like to leave with you today is when you are going through tough seasons, a bump in the road, or even setbacks.

Remember what Paul tells us in Romans, that ALL things are working together for our good, and come to an understanding that your current situation won't always be a reflection of your final destination. But stay steadfast knowing that in the end, just like the cake you will rise into what you were created to be.

I want to encourage you to be strong and stay put in the pain! It's supposed to be there, not necessarily to scare you but to strengthen you. There is something on the other side waiting for you that requires more than what you possess right now.

Although you may see it as wrongdoings and affliction towards you, we must remember that God sees what we can't see, he hears the conversations that we don't hear, and he keeps us put until the crooked path is straight!

What we see as suffering God sees as opportunity. What we see as pain God sees as possibility. The structure of our human nature only allows us to see things in the present as what they are. But God is omniscient which means he knows everything today, yesterday, and tomorrow!

God is metamorphosing YOU into NEW!

Prayer:

Heavenly Father,

As we come before you in prayer, we acknowledge the reality of pain in our lives. Lord, we understand that pain is an inescapable part of our earthly existence, touching every aspect of our being. Yet, in the midst of this, we find hope and purpose in Your Word.

Thank you for the message of "Purposeful Pain" that the Apostle Paul shares with the Christian community in Romans 8:28. We are comforted by the assurance that all things work together for the good of those who love You and are called according to Your purpose.

In our journey through pain—whether physical, relational, mental, emotional, financial, or spiritual—we seek Your guidance and strength. Like the ingredients in a recipe, which on their own may seem tasteless or undesirable, we trust that You are orchestrating a masterpiece in our lives.

Just as a cake rises and transforms in the oven, may we rise from our trials and be transformed into what You created us to be. Help us to see beyond our present circumstances and understand that our current situation does not define our final destination.

Lord, when life's challenges seem overwhelming, remind us that what we perceive as suffering, You see as an opportunity. What we see as pain, You see as possibility. Strengthen us to endure, knowing that You are working in us, shaping us into something new.

We thank You for the promise that there is something on the other side of our pain, something that requires more than what we possess right now. Help us to trust Your omniscient perspective, knowing that You are leading us through a process of metamorphosis. In Jesus name we pray, Amen!

The key points of this message entitled "Purposeful Pain" are as follows:

1. **Introduction:** The message acknowledges that pain is an inevitable part of life, stemming from various sources such as physical, relational, emotional, financial, and spiritual challenges. It emphasizes that everyone faces pain at some point in life.

2. **Scripture Reference:** The message references Romans 8:28, which states, "For we know that all things work together for the good of those who love God and who are called according to his purpose." This verse is presented as a source of encouragement and guidance for believers.

3. **Apostle Paul's Message:** The apostle Paul's message to the Christian church is highlighted. He offers direction, encouragement, and guidance to the believers, assuring them that even in the face of adversity, God can use all circumstances for good, both in their lives and in the world.

4. **Baking Analogy:** The message uses an analogy involving baking to illustrate the concept of various individual ingredients

coming together to create something delicious. It emphasizes that the final result is not determined by the taste of individual ingredients but by their combination.

5. **Message of Hope:** The message encourages readers to find hope and strength in difficult seasons, bumps in the road, or setbacks. It suggests that just as ingredients come together to create something delightful, all life experiences, including pain, work together for one's ultimate purpose and growth.

6. **Staying Strong in Pain:** Readers are encouraged to stay strong and endure pain because it is meant to strengthen them, not scare them. The devotional suggests that what may seem like suffering and affliction to individuals is seen as opportunity and possibility by God.

7. **God's Perspective:** The message emphasizes that God's perspective is different from human understanding. While humans may see suffering and pain, God sees the potential for transformation and growth. God knows the past, present, and future and is working to mold individuals into something new.

8. **Metamorphosis:** The message concludes by highlighting that God is transforming individuals into something new. It emphasizes that what may be perceived as suffering is part of the process of becoming what one was created to be.

9. **Closing Prayer:** The message concludes with a prayer thanking God for the message and praying for a safe and productive week for the readers.

Overall, this message conveys the message that pain and challenges in life have a purpose, and God can use them for good in the lives of those who love Him and are called according to His purpose. It encourages readers to stay strong in the midst of difficulties, knowing that God's perspective and plans are far greater than human understanding.

Return To Me

This message is entitled "Return To Me."

After graduating high school, I got a job working for a great brother of mine's A/C company. The more I worked there, the more people I met, the more knowledge I gained, the more opportunities I embarked on, and the more money I made.

I was making so much money to the point that I was spending more money in a day than most people in my neighborhood made in a month. As time progressed, the want and hunger for money became stronger day after day. It became so contagious to the point that I'd go days without reading my Bible (which I usually read multiple times a day), and occasionally I would skip Wednesday and Thursday night Bible studies (which I usually never miss).

I guess it's safe to say that in a way I dethroned God and made money my master.

After about a solid 2 weeks, I felt the absence of God's presence (which I usually feel all the time) in my daily life.

Although I was making all this money and had access to do and buy anything I wanted (externally)… I didn't feel the potent flow of abundance that made me feel free (internally).

Everything you could possibly imagine that could go wrong went wrong. Before you knew it, my vehicle started acting up, bills started to get higher, expenses started to come out of nowhere, and the money started to run dry.

This then made me question… God, I have all these things going on, and I'm praying, but it feels as if you left me…

You know, this reminds me of when the Lord spoke to the prophet Zechariah in chapter one of the book of Zechariah. He was furious with the people because they had started to reject Him. So, God spoke and said that if the people returned to Him, He would do the same for them and embrace them.

Verse 3 of Chapter 1 reads… "So tell the people, this is what the Lord of armies says: return to me- this is the declaration of the Lord of armies- and I will return to you, says the Lord of armies."

The Lord claimed that He had forewarned their ancestors to turn away from their sinful behavior, and how they disregarded his advice and had to deal with the results of their actions.

Zechariah was particularly concerned that the people's reaction to the Lord come from their hearts and not just be an outward display of repentance, as it had been so frequently with their forefathers.

He, therefore, urged them to consider what transpired when their ancestors cried out to God in their misery. They continued to act idolatrous and immoral after the Lord answered their petitions.

Now Zechariah's message is very clear to them. God said to return to me (not just to the land), And if they did God said (I will return to you).

Friends, we must acknowledge that this still holds true today. When we have broken our relationship with God by sin, we cannot deceive ourselves into believing that we are walking with him. We turn from God because of sin. Therefore, it is our responsibility to come back to God and ask for His grace and mercy.

Zechariah uses historical examples to encourage people to turn back to the Lord. The warnings of God's prophets about impending judgment will certainly come to pass if the people do not repent. Therefore, it is imperative that God's people repent and restore the temple of the Lord.

As time progresses, it is so easy to become distracted and tempted to fall off the road of righteousness. But this text, like many others, demonstrates that the ticket issued to board the train of forgiveness is repentance.

And luckily for you, The Lord's ears are always turned your way, and his arms are always opened.

Prayer:

Gracious Heavenly Father,

We come before You with humble hearts, acknowledging Your sovereignty and grace. Lord, thank you for the powerful message of "Return To Me." In the midst of the distractions and temptations of life, help us to remain grounded in our faith and devotion to You.

We confess that, at times, we may inadvertently dethrone You from the throne of our hearts, allowing other desires, such as the pursuit of wealth or worldly success, to take precedence. Like the prodigal son, we may find ourselves straying away from Your presence, feeling the void that comes with the absence of Your peace and abundance.

We are reminded of the words You spoke to the prophet Zechariah, urging the people to return to You. Your promise echoes through the ages, "Return to me, and I will return to you." Lord, we seek Your forgiveness for the times we have turned away, and we earnestly desire to return to Your loving embrace.

Just as You warned the ancestors of the consequences of their sinful behavior, we understand that our actions have repercussions. In moments of distress and hardship, when we question Your presence, help us to remember that it is our own choices that can distance us from You.

Lord, grant us the wisdom to learn from historical examples and to recognize the importance of genuine repentance. May our turning back to You be heartfelt and sincere, not just an outward display. We acknowledge that true restoration comes through repentance, and we submit ourselves to Your mercy and grace. In Jesus name we pray, Amen!

The key points of this message entitled "Return To Me" are as follows:

1. **Personal Experience**: The author shares their personal journey after high school, where they began working and accumulating wealth, which led to a focus on materialism and neglect of their spiritual life.
2. **Money as Master**: They discuss how their pursuit of money became all-consuming, to the point where they neglected reading the Bible and missed Bible studies.
3. **Feeling God's Absence**: The author reflects on the feeling of God's absence in their life after prioritizing money over their relationship with God.
4. **Reference to Zechariah**: The message references the story of the prophet Zechariah in the Bible, where God called upon the people to return to Him.
5. **Importance of Repentance**: The message emphasizes the importance of genuine repentance and returning to God when one has strayed from their faith.
6. **Historical Examples**: The message encourages readers to learn from historical examples in the Bible and understand the consequences of not turning back to God.
7. **God's Open Arms**: It reminds readers that God is always ready to welcome those who seek Him, emphasizing His grace and mercy.
8. **Prayer**: The message ends with a prayer for those who may feel they have strayed too far from God, encouraging them to return to Him, as there is no such thing as "too late" in God's eyes.

Overall, this message draws attention to the importance of prioritizing one's relationship with God over material pursuits and highlights the message of repentance and God's willingness to embrace those who turn back to Him.

Righteous Suffering

Job, who is considered the greatest man, a sinless man among all the people of the East (Job 1:3), was stripped of his family and health by direct satanic attacks. Scriptures teach us that the Sabeans, the Chaldeans, and Satan himself all had a part in striking down his servants, taking his cattle, and killing his children.

Now, one would think, how could God allow this to happen to a man like Job? How could you be such a faithful steward/servant of the Lord, and something like this were to happen?

After reading the text, you might think that Job would grow angry and disconnect all trust in the Lord.

Nevertheless, despite all that happened to Job, he stood up, tore his robe, and shaved his head. He fell to the ground and worshiped, saying, "Naked I came from my mother's womb, and naked I will leave this life. The Lord gives, and the Lord takes away. Blessed be the name of the Lord" (Job 1:20-21).

This message is entitled "Righteous Suffering."

The thing I find most interesting about Job's life, especially earlier in the book, is that he was a just man! As a matter of fact, he is as righteous and faithful as they come.

But although that may be the case, his righteousness and faithfulness didn't exempt him from suffering.

These past two months have been the most painful and difficult 60 days I've ever embarked on.

Speaking for myself here, I eat, breathe, and sleep the word of God. I hunger for his heart day in and day out, and I dedicate hours out of my day to worship, honor, talk to, and glorify him.

I talk on radio shows about his goodness, speak at events about his everlasting peace, host bible studies, and lead peers of all ages, backgrounds, and ethnicities to his never-ending love. I've created and been on podcasts expressing who he is and what he has done for me and what he can do for other people. I'm in the process of writing another book that shows how to use him in your everyday business, social, and relational lives. I created this devotional you are hearing me speak on right now on his behalf, along with a clothing line from which the source to fund it is straight out of my pocket. BUT YET... I'm not exempt from suffering.

It all started in early May of 2023 right after my college finals when I got the news that someone I was very close to tragically passed away exactly a month before I was supposed to see them. A week later I was driving, and my vehicle started smoking, and next thing you know, I was vehicle-less and later found out that I needed a brand-new engine. On top of that, due to unprecedented circumstances, I then became unemployed.

Eventually, I was in a position where bills were coming in, with no way of getting around anywhere, trying to make ends meet, and making sure that my future endeavors were still intact. I found myself relating to Job and grew a personal relationship with him through the text as he showed me what it is like to be a righteous sufferer but to also remain high in my faith and stay devoted to the Lord!

Just like Job, I experienced what it was like to remain steadfast in the Lord while also being under attack by Satan's attempts to tempt me into falling for wickedness.

There were plenty of moments where I had the direct opportunity to allow what Satan was doing externally to misguide and redirect me from what God was doing inside of me internally.

But just like Job, when all hell was breaking loose, and when everything that could possibly go wrong goes wrong... through agony and affliction, through pain and turmoil, through just and unjust, I got down on my knees and proclaimed (in today's terms)....

Naked I come from my mother's womb. And naked I will leave this life. The Lord gives, And the Lord takes away. Blessed be the Name of the Lord.

As Christians today, we can be victorious over Satan if we take advantage of the protection available through our personal relationship with the Lord Jesus Christ.

Satan is REAL and wants to spread his wicked influence over everyone. God restrains him despite his strength. He can only be in one location at once and has no knowledge of the future other than what God has already recorded.

God "placed a hedge around" Job and his family, as the saying goes. Satan could not directly attack him, who, while not sinless, lived a flawless and honest life, until God took away that defense.

All of Job's actions and interactions were characterized by his moral and spiritual purity. Even after losing his family and his health, he refused to place the blame on God, despite his wife's advice to "curse God and die!" (Chapter 2:9–10)

By utilizing the protection provided by our close personal relationship with the Lord Jesus Christ, we may overcome Satan as Christians in today's world. Just as Paul wrote in (Ephesians 6:10-11) Finally, be strengthened by the Lord and by his vast strength. Put on the full armor of God so that you can stand against the schemes of the devil.

The Holy Spirit wants us to be aware that Satan is strong and wants us to sin against God, so He oversaw the writing of the Book of Job. But this story's main goal is not to illustrate that. Instead, Job's overall responses show us that it is possible to remain devoted to God despite the tough circumstances of life, including explicit satanic attacks and God's seeming silence.

And maybe you're just like I was... Maybe you can relate to Job because you know what it's like to be in a season of righteous suffering.

But regardless of what comes your way you know who your God is. You know that he is faithful regardless of what is going on around you. You have seen him show up and show out, make ways out of no ways, and perform miracles unknown and unseen to the human eye. Just like Job, you can proclaim on your knees that Naked I come from my Mother's Womb, and naked I will leave this life. For the Lord gives, and the Lord takes away, Blessed be the Name of the Lord.

Prayer:

Heavenly Father,

As we bow before You in prayer, we are reminded of the message on "Righteous Suffering." The story of Job, a righteous man who endured unimaginable trials and suffering, teaches us profound lessons about faith and trust in You.

Lord, we acknowledge that suffering is a part of our human experience, and sometimes, like Job, we find ourselves in seasons of righteous suffering. In those moments, when our world seems to crumble around us, help us, like Job, to stand firm in our faith.

We lift up those who are currently going through trials, facing challenges, and experiencing suffering. May they find solace in the example of Job, who, despite his losses and pain, remained steadfast in his devotion to You.

Lord, we confess that, in our own lives, we may encounter difficulties that test our faith. Grant us the strength to echo Job's words, "Naked I came from my mother's womb, and naked I will leave this life. The Lord gives, and the Lord takes away. Blessed be the Name of the Lord."

We pray for the courage to worship You even in the midst of adversity, to trust Your plan, and to remain devoted to You. Like Job, may we recognize that Satan may try to bring affliction and suffering, but through our personal relationship with Jesus Christ, we can overcome. In Jesus name we pray, Amen!

The key points of this message entitled "Righteous Suffering" are as follows:

1. **Introduction:** The message begins by introducing the concept of righteous suffering and its relation to the biblical story of Job. It mentions that Job, a righteous and faithful man, experienced immense suffering and loss, which raises questions about why God allows such suffering.
2. **Job's Story:** The message briefly outlines Job's background as a man considered the greatest among the people of the East, known for his righteousness and faithfulness. It highlights that Job faced a series of tragic events, including the loss of his family, health, and possessions, due to direct Satanic attacks.
3. **Job's Response:** Despite the overwhelming suffering and loss, Job's response is one of reverence and worship to God. He tears his robe, shaves his head, falls to the ground, and acknowledges God's sovereignty, saying, "Naked I came from my mother's womb, and naked I will leave this life. The LORD gives, and the LORD takes away. Blessed be the name of the LORD" (Job 1:20-21).
4. **Personal Connection:** The author shares a personal experience of going through a period of intense suffering and challenges in their own life. They relate to Job's experience of remaining steadfast in faith despite hardships.

5. **Understanding Righteous Suffering:** The message emphasizes that righteous suffering can happen to anyone, regardless of their faith and dedication to God. It raises questions about why God allows suffering but highlights that Job's story demonstrates the possibility of remaining devoted to God even in challenging circumstances.

6. **Spiritual Protection:** The message briefly discusses Satan's role in causing suffering and how Christians can be protected through their personal relationship with the Lord Jesus Christ. It references Ephesians 6:10-11, which encourages believers to put on the full armor of God to stand against the schemes of the devil.

7. **Encouragement:** The message encourages readers who may be going through seasons of righteous suffering to remember that God is faithful and can work miracles even in challenging circumstances. It reaffirms the proclamation made by Job, expressing trust in God's sovereignty and goodness.

8. **Final Prayer:** The message concludes with a prayer, thanking God for the message and asking that it inspires and encourages those who read it.

Overall, this message explores the theme of righteous suffering, drawing inspiration from the biblical story of Job and emphasizing the importance of maintaining faith and trust in God during difficult times.

Step Into Your Destiny

Isaiah 43:18-19 "Do not remember the former things, nor consider the things of old. Behold, I will do a new thing; now it shall spring forth; Shall you not know it?"

This message is entitled 'Step into Your Destiny.'

Stop allowing the pain of the past to get in the way of the fruit of the future.

Often, we allow what happened in the past to affect what is now happening in the present, which will eventually sabotage what's supposed to happen in the future.

For some of my fellows out there, we have programmed our minds not to trust the entire gender of women because of the few that broke our hearts...

For some of my ladies out there, we have created a blockage or some sort of wall to prevent being 100% committed to a man due to past experiences with bad men. There are some of us out here who won't dare try to start that business back up or try again for another child because the expectations of what was supposed to happen didn't meet the reality of what was actually happening.

Believe it or not, when this starts to happen, Satan will use what hurt you or what didn't go your way to distract you from God's will and promises over your life.

Have you ever talked to someone and tried to give them great advice that can be 100% accurate in accordance with the season they are currently in, and they use what happened to them, or what someone said to them, or how something didn't work out back then as an excuse not to execute your prophecy?

Or have you yourself ever been in a situation where a great opportunity has exposed itself to you, and you are excited about it and considering trying it out, and then out of nowhere you get blindsided by bad memories or hateful thoughts that discourage you from taking the opportunity?

Or maybe you're just like Peter when he saw Jesus walking on water and wanted to walk as well. Jesus said, 'Come to me.' As Peter began taking his first steps, it all looked clear and promising, but then Peter, being human, came to his worldly reality, knowing that man can't walk on water. He became so consumed by what was happening around him that he lost his sight and vision of who was standing right in front of him.

Could it be that maybe it is not for you, or is it more so that Satan is trying to use your painful moments as a mental fog to make you think that you have no destiny?

There's a purpose attached to the reasoning of me sharing Isaiah chapter 43, verses 18 through 19 with you at the beginning. And that purpose is exactly what it reads. God is saying I rescued you from sin and slavery. I prevented your death by intervening.

However, the goal is not to be freed from slavery or to live. I have something greater and different for you, but it will necessitate that you continue onward despite being in hostile environments, and as you walk in obedience to Me, you are continuously moving away from what was and moving toward what will be.

Friends, listen to me, and if you think I'm talking to you, then I am!

It's time to let go! It's time to move on! It's time to get your joy back! God is ready to spring you forth into something beyond your mental capacity! Something so pure and so potent that you never knew existed!

Get out of the past and step into your destiny!

Prayer:

Heavenly Father,

We humbly come before you with hearts open to your transformative power. We thank you for the powerful message of "Step into Your Destiny" and the reminder from Isaiah 43:18-19 to let go of the past and embrace the new thing you have for us.

Lord, we confess that at times we allow the pain of our past to overshadow the potential of our future. We build walls and barriers based on past hurts and disappointments, hindering us from fully stepping into the destiny you have prepared for us.

Today, we surrender those past hurts and negative experiences to you. We ask for your healing touch to mend the wounds and scars that have influenced our choices and decisions. Help us break free from the chains of past pain and disappointment.

We acknowledge that Satan often uses our past to distract us from your will and promises over our lives. Give us the strength and discernment to recognize when the enemy is trying to cloud our vision and discourage us from stepping into the destiny you have ordained for us.

As we move forward, may the power of your Holy Spirit guide our steps. May we not be paralyzed by fear, doubt, or past experiences, but rather, embolden us to trust in your promises and move forward with faith. In Jesus name we pray, Amen!

The key points of this message entitled "Step into Your Destiny" are as follows:

1. **Scriptural Reference:** The message starts with a reference to Isaiah 43:18-19, emphasizing the message of not dwelling on the past but looking forward to the new things that God has in store.

2. **The Impact of the Past:** The message highlights how people often allow past hurts, disappointments, and failures to affect their present and future decisions. This can lead to a lack of trust, fear, and hesitation.

3. **Satan's Distraction:** It points out that Satan can use these past experiences and negative thoughts to distract individuals from God's will and promises for their lives. The devotional suggests that Satan can hinder people from executing God's plans by reminding them of their past.

4. **Overcoming Negative Thoughts:** The message mentions situations where individuals are discouraged from pursuing opportunities or acting on good advice due to negative memories or thoughts. It encourages readers to overcome these obstacles.

5. **Peter Walking on Water:** The story of Peter walking on water with Jesus is used as an example of how individuals can become consumed by their worldly realities and lose sight of their destiny when they focus on their past experiences.

6. **God's Greater Plan:** The message reminds readers that God has something greater and different in store for them. It emphasizes that God wants people to move away from their past and move toward what He has prepared for their future.

7. **Letting Go and Moving On:** The core message is that it's time to let go of the past, move on, and regain joy. The devotional encourages readers to step into their destiny, acknowledging that their past doesn't define them and that God determines their identity.

8. **Prayer:** The message concludes with a prayer asking God for the strength to let go of the past, move forward into their

destiny, and reclaim joy. It also prays for the readers' clarity and determination to embrace what God has in store for them.

Overall, this message reflects the importance of not allowing past experiences to hinder one's future and encourages readers to trust in God's plan and purpose for their lives. It calls for a release of the past and a step into a brighter future filled with God's blessings and destiny.

The Gift Of Grace

Today, I want to delve into the astounding notion that grace is a gift. In the spiritual sense, grace is frequently referred to as undeserved favor, a deed of kindness, or heavenly love and forgiveness bestowed upon us by the Lord. It is a beautiful and transformative gift that we receive without deserving it.

This message is entitled "The Gift Of Grace."

It can be challenging to understand the concept of receiving something for free in a society that frequently emphasizes performance, merit, and achievement. But grace serves as a reminder that we don't have to work for God's love and favor. It is freely given to us, not because of our goodness or deeds, but rather because of the generosity of a kind and compassionate God.

An example that I love to use when discussing this topic is comparing a trophy with a present. Perhaps you remember when you were younger and competed in sports. At the end of every match or game, there was always a trophy presentation, and that trophy wasn't for just anybody; it had to be earned. You may also recall Christmas morning, sitting by the tree with your family, unwrapping gifts. Someone would hand it to you, and it was yours to keep. You didn't have to work for it or compete to get it; it was just given to you out of the kindness of someone else's heart because they love you. Notice how both examples ended with a reward, but one was earned, and the other was gifted.

Believe it or not, when it comes to grace, you don't have to compete or work for it. It is God's gift to you as a reflection of His love towards you despite your sin. Most of us would rather earn rewards than receive gifts.

As a word of caution, we must refrain from making prayer into a task. The reality is that everything nice and spiritual must be transformed into labor due to the constant pull of our flesh. The act of working appeals to the flesh because it satisfies our need for pride. Most of us prefer to earn rewards rather than receive gifts. But, as we've seen, grace needs to be accepted as a gift.

The Bible is filled with passages that emphasize the gift of grace. One of the most well-known verses is Ephesians 2:8-9 (NIV): "For you are saved by grace through faith, and this is not from yourselves; it is God's gift— 9 not from works, so that no one can boast." This verse underscores that grace is not a reward for our actions but a gift we receive through faith.

Grace offers us a new beginning and the ability to be forgiven for our mistakes. It serves as a reminder of the love and forgiveness shown to us, rather than our past defining who we are. Even in the depths of our hopelessness, it is a gift that brings hope.

Grace should also not be kept to oneself. It is a gift that should be distributed. We are obligated to show people grace in the same way that we have received it. When we do, we transform into conduits for the love and mercy of God, inspiring compassion and forgiveness throughout our societies and the entirety of the planet.

Therefore, while we consider the idea of grace as a gift, let us keep in mind that it is a strong divine force that surpasses our limitations. It challenges us to live with appreciation, humility, and an open heart while serving as a reminder of the limitless love of God. We experience the transforming power of a gift that can influence both our lives and the lives of people around us when we receive and give grace.

Hebrews 4:16 is a verse from the New Testament that references grace, and it reads: "Let us then approach God's throne of grace with confidence, so that we may receive mercy and find grace to help us in our time of need." This verse encourages us to approach God with confidence, knowing that we can find mercy and grace in times of need. It also emphasizes the idea that we can have a close and personal relationship with God while seeking His help and forgiveness with confidence and trusting in His love and compassion.

Friends, as I articulated earlier, grace isn't earned; it's given! Walk knowing that regardless of what you've done, who you've wronged, or even what you think. None of that can get in the way of God's love for you and receiving His grace.

Prayer:

Heavenly Father,

We come before You with hearts full of gratitude for the profound gift of grace. Today, we reflect on the concept that grace is not earned but freely given—a reflection of Your undeserved favor, kindness, and heavenly love.

In a world that often emphasizes performance and achievement, grace serves as a powerful reminder that Your love and favor are bestowed upon us not because of our goodness or deeds but because of Your generosity. We are recipients of a beautiful and transformative gift that we could never earn on our own.

Lord, we are reminded of the analogy of a trophy and a present. Help us to understand that grace is not a trophy to be earned through competition or merit. Instead, it is a gift, freely given out of the kindness of Your heart because You love us. Just as we receive gifts on Christmas morning without having to work for them, so too do we receive the gift of Your grace.

Father, guard us against turning prayer into a task, and help us accept the gift of grace with open hearts. May we resist the temptation to rely on our works and understand that grace is meant to be accepted, not earned.

Your Word in Ephesians 2:8-9 reminds us that we are saved by grace through faith, and this is not from ourselves; it is Your gift, not from works, so that no one can boast. May this truth anchor our understanding of grace, keeping us humble and appreciative of Your unmerited favor.

Hebrews 4:16 encourages us to approach Your throne of grace with confidence, knowing that we can receive mercy and find grace to help us in our time of need. May we boldly come before You, trusting in Your boundless love and compassion. In Jesus name we pray, Amen!

The key points of this message entitled "The Gift of Grace" are as follows:

1. **Definition of Grace**: The message starts by defining grace as undeserved favor, a deed of kindness, or heavenly love and forgiveness bestowed upon us by the Lord. It emphasizes that grace is a beautiful and transformative gift that we receive without deserving it.
2. **Gift vs. Reward**: The message explores the distinction between earning a reward through merit and receiving a gift. It uses examples of earning a trophy versus receiving a Christmas gift to illustrate the concept that grace is freely given and not something we work for or compete to attain.
3. **Caution against Making Prayer a Task**: The message cautions against turning prayer into a task or work, as our human nature often seeks to earn or achieve. It highlights that grace is a gift that must be accepted rather than earned.
4. **Biblical References to Grace**: The message references Ephesians 2:8-9, a well-known verse that emphasizes that grace is not a reward for our actions, but a gift received through faith. It points out that grace offers a new beginning, forgiveness, and hope.
5. **Sharing Grace**: Grace is portrayed as a gift meant to be shared. The message encourages readers to show grace to others in the same way they have received it, becoming channels for God's love and mercy.

6. **Approaching God's Throne of Grace**: Hebrews 4:16 is mentioned as a verse that encourages believers to approach God with confidence to receive His mercy and grace in times of need.

7. **Closing Prayer**: The message closes with a prayer expressing gratitude for the gift of grace, the release of guilt and humiliation, and a commitment to live in response to God's love and grace.

Overall, the fruits of this message is that grace is a gift freely given by God, and we are called to accept it with humility and gratitude, share it with others, and approach God confidently to receive His grace in times of need.

The Who Behind The Why!

Oftentimes in life, we all face some sort of catastrophe. For some of us, we see these so-called catastrophes in our lives more frequently than others. A few examples of catastrophes could be a death in the family, eviction from your place of residence, a loss of a job, or even a harsh breakup or divorce. The severity of these catastrophes, when they happen, can cause you to question why God allowed it.

This message is entitled "The Who Behind The Why."

The year was 2020. Hypothetically speaking, 2020 was the worst year of many of our lives. This 12-month span brought social injustices, political corruption, and the most popular catastrophe: COVID-19!

Significant hardship was brought on by the COVID-19 pandemic and its associated economic effects. Tens of millions of individuals lost their employment in the first few months of the crisis. Within a few months, employment started to increase again, but unemployment remained high throughout 2020. The exceedingly high levels of hardship experienced in the summer of 2020 were significantly reduced by increased employment and high alleviation initiatives. Near the end of 2021, there were still a lot of unmet needs, with 10 million homes having unpaid rent and 20 million households saying that they hadn't had enough to eat in the previous seven days. Approximately 3 million fewer people were working in early 2022 than they were before the pandemic, despite gradual progress, notably in recent months.

COVID-19 was arguably charted as the worst thing to happen in human history! I remember it all just like it was yesterday. Turning on the news, you saw people dying by the hundreds worldwide every single day. It felt like as the days progressed, you didn't know who would be breathing the next day in your household.

This then left many people asking this one question... Why?

Lord, this virus killed my husband or my wife. Why would you allow this to happen to me?

Lord, my mom had an underlying condition and got COVID and passed away. Why would you allow this to happen to me?

Lord, my best friend for 20 years had all the boosters, wore her mask everywhere, and was quarantined, and she still died from this virus. Lord, why?

And sometimes when the why is happening, it feels as if the who is not present. But what if I told you that the who is present? What if I told you that God was there the whole time?

Friends, sometimes God permits catastrophes in our lives because they reveal him to us in ways we have never known him before. Sometimes God allows, produces, and causes catastrophes to show that he alone is God and will cause divine disruption to the world in order to implement something new. When he wants you to go to the next level of connection with him, he will typically use some sort of crisis or catastrophe.

In the book of Exodus, God led the Israelites to come up against the Red Sea when they were trying to cross it as they made their journey from Egypt to the Promised Land. But by letting them come to the end of themselves, he also gave them the chance to see what he was capable of when there were no other options left.

Would you believe me if I told you that God does some of his best work when your back is against the wall?

I remember when COVID-19 was at its forefront, and it seemed that there was nothing anyone could do to prevent, control, and stop it. I then started to see people call out to the Lord like never before.

He will use these catastrophes so that you may cry out to him and witness his glory, power, and presence.

While most of us assume that blessings only come in the form of grace and good doings, God teaches and demonstrates that he is also capable of benefiting us through suffering and pain.

A decline in your circumstances may sometimes be a blessing in disguise since it sets you up for an upturn. The Israelites' increased workload as Egyptian slaves is what led to their cries for help from God. This prompted him to hear their cries and eventually brought about their freedom and establishment as a separate nation.

The goal of this message is to give you a comprehensive understanding that you are just a cry-out away. Leave this message knowing that the ticket issued to board the train of blessings is simply a cry out to the Lord.

Prayer:

Heavenly Father,

We come before you with humble hearts, acknowledging the challenges and catastrophes we face in life. In times of hardship and confusion, we often find ourselves questioning the reasons behind the pain and suffering. Today, we seek clarity and understanding through the message of "The Who Behind The Why."

Lord, the year 2020 brought unprecedented challenges, and the COVID-19 pandemic became a global catastrophe that shook the foundations of our lives. Many faced loss, grief, and uncertainty, prompting us to ask, "Why, Lord?" In those moments of despair, it may have felt as if you were distant or absent.

But today, we are reminded that you are the "Who" behind the "Why." Even in the midst of catastrophes, you are present, working in ways we may not fully comprehend. Your Word teaches us that sometimes you permit crises to reveal yourself to us in ways we've never known before.

Just as you led the Israelites to the Red Sea, allowing them to come to the end of themselves, you demonstrated your power and glory when there seemed to be no other way. You do some of your best work when our backs are against the wall. Help us trust that even in the darkest moments, you are orchestrating a divine disruption to bring about something new.

Lord, when catastrophes occur, may we cry out to you and witness your glory, power, and presence. Help us understand that a decline in circumstances can sometimes be a blessing in disguise, setting us up for an upturn. Just as the Israelites' cries led to their freedom, we believe that our cries for help will be heard by you. In Jesus name we pray, Amen!

The key points of this message entitled "The Who Behind The Why" are as follows:

1. **Introduction to Catastrophes:** The message starts by acknowledging that everyone faces catastrophes in life, such as the loss of a loved one, eviction, job loss, or a difficult breakup, which can lead to questions about why God allows such hardships.
2. **The Context of 2020:** The message reflects on the year 2020, particularly the challenges brought by the COVID-19 pandemic. It highlights the economic and emotional hardships experienced by many during this time.
3. **Questioning "Why?":** The message shares the questions and doubts people often have when faced with tragic events, wondering why God would allow such suffering and loss.
4. **The "Who" Behind the "Why":** The central message of the devotional is that even in times of catastrophe, God is present.

It suggests that God may permit crises to reveal Himself to us in new and profound ways.

5. **Divine Disruption:** It suggests that God can use catastrophes to disrupt the ordinary course of events in our lives and to lead us to a deeper connection with Him.

6. **Blessings through Suffering:** The message challenges the notion that blessings only come through grace and good times, stating that God can also bless us through suffering and pain. It cites the example of the Israelites' suffering as slaves in Egypt, which ultimately led to their freedom.

7. **The Power of Crying Out:** The message concludes by emphasizing the importance of crying out to God in times of need, as it can be a ticket to experiencing His blessings and presence.

8. **Prayer:** The message ends with a prayer, expressing gratitude for the message and asking for God's presence and blessings for those who feel alone in their struggles.

Overall, this message seeks to provide a perspective on catastrophes, suggesting that even in the midst of difficult times, God is present and may be working to deepen our connection with Him and ultimately bring blessings out of hardship. It encourages readers to turn to God and trust that there is a purpose and a "who" behind the "why" of their trials.

Unsinkable Faith

———

Have you ever been in a position where your faith has to be the driving point of your life?

Have you ever experienced a season when God is calling you to a very large task, and the only point of direction was the sound of His voice? Maybe you know what it's like to be in such a position while also having to lead your family and your ministry at the same time. All this while being ridiculed by others because the foreignness of what God is telling you to do isn't exactly logical in the context of the present day and time.

If this is you, I want you to go with me to the book of Genesis as we dive into Noah's story and get a comprehensive understanding of what it really means to obey at the forefront of destruction!

This message is entitled "Unsinkable Faith."

The story of Noah and the Flood is one of judgment and salvation, of obedience and disobedience. Noah was a righteous and blameless man among his contemporaries. He walked with God throughout his days on earth, which, at the time, was wicked and corrupt. Noah distinguished himself by leading a good life in a time of destruction.

Noah was probably made fun of for building a huge boat when no flood had yet been witnessed on Earth. Nevertheless, he didn't care what other people thought. He only obeyed God's directions with a willing heart and hands, demonstrating the building of an Ark. He was protected from destruction because God rewarded him for his righteousness and faithfulness.

Now, by faith, Noah, being divinely forewarned of things not yet seen, moved with godly fear, and prepared an ark for the saving of his household, by which he condemned the world and became an heir of the righteousness that is according to faith. This verse first explains the warning that Noah's faith took to heart. When Noah lived, there was a shocking lack of respect for God. When there is no fear of God, that is a sign of a dying civilization.

But Noah feared God and showed it by acting in accordance with godly understanding and wisdom. If we fear God, it will also be evident in our worship, salvation, assurance, discernment, and deliverance. This text also illustrates the results of Noah's faith. Being a man of faith, Noah followed God's command and started building the ark before he even witnessed the flood.

Now, it amazes me how Noah strictly follows the commands of the Lord while building this Ark with no clear signs that a flood is on its way. As a matter of fact, this is a teaching moment for us… using an example of this in today's world… It's the middle of July in Texas, and God tells you to make and buy as many coats as you possibly can and tell everyone else to do the same because there is going to be a huge snowstorm on July 27th.

So now you and your kids are out doing what he said, and everyone is talking about you and calling you crazy because it's the summertime and it is not logical that a snowstorm will come in the hottest month of the year on one day. Now, July 27th comes around, the sky starts to get dark, and the temperatures start to drop drastically, and because you obeyed the Lord's command, you and your kids survive the storm while everyone else dies of frostbite.

Now back to Noah's Journey… To finish their work, Noah and his sons needed to be patient. They had to toil while being constantly seen and maybe laughed at by those who would pass them as they worked and would shake their heads and openly mock them.

On a quick side note…remember, up until the very end of Christ's earthly life, when those threats were fulfilled, Jesus and his followers were likewise rejected and threatened with bodily harm. They could identify with Noah, who was an outcast and a laughingstock.

To take it back to the text, what he experienced served as a reminder to Noah that he not only required light, but that God had already incorporated light into his plans for Noah's future in this small area at the top of his floating world. The world needed light, not just for Noah.

We today can get a glimpse of what that really entails through Noah's Ark. Despite not being sinless, God saved Noah because of his faithfulness. His "faith was counted to him as righteousness", just like it was for Abraham in Romans. Just as Noah waited for the light to reflect from a dripping mountain peak coming out of the water, so it is with Christians today as they wait for Christ to return.

God gave the order, and Noah followed it, constructed the Ark, filled it with animals, shut the doors, and the water rose around him. The entire earth vanished. He had to wait for approximately a year after the first rain before a dove came and gave him an olive branch to indicate that the land had returned.

As God forewarned Noah's people, the same sins committed in Noah's day continue to be committed today. He has also forewarned us. The wealth that Noah's faith attracted is finally revealed. Noah left a legacy of righteousness; despite his obedience, he was eventually redeemed by God's favor rather than by his own efforts.

In the midst of our generation's rebellion, we can lead our families into the ark of safety, which is a representation of Jesus Christ, by imitating Noah's act of confidence in God. Just as Christ seals our salvation, God sealed Noah within the ark. Use it in your life. Do you, just like Noah, lead your family with unwavering faith? Do you feel moved to fear and follow God? If not, establish God as the head of your life and household today.

Prayer:

Heavenly Father,

As we gather in prayer, we reflect on the message of "Unsinkable Faith" and the inspiring journey of Noah. In moments when faith becomes the driving force of our lives, and we are called to tasks seemingly illogical to the world, may we draw strength from Noah's unwavering commitment to obeying Your voice.

Noah, in the face of ridicule, followed Your divine instructions with a willing heart and hands, building an ark to save his household. Lord, grant us the same courage to obey, even when we cannot see the signs or the logic behind Your commands.

May we, like Noah, fear You and demonstrate this fear through our worship, salvation, assurance, discernment, and deliverance. In times when our faith is tested, help us to act in godly understanding and wisdom.

In the midst of a world that lacks respect for You, let our faith be a shining light that condemns the darkness. Like Noah, help us to act in faith before witnessing the flood, trusting in Your divine plan.

Just as Noah and his sons toiled patiently while being mocked, may we persevere in obedience, even when others question our actions. As we face ridicule and challenges, grant us the strength to hold onto the promises You have spoken to us.

Remind us, O Lord, that, like Noah, we may be outcasts and laughingstocks in the eyes of the world, but our focus is on You. In our journey, may we find patience and endurance, knowing that even Christ and His followers faced rejection and threats.

As Noah waited for the light to reflect from a dripping mountain peak, we too wait for the return of Christ. Let our faith be counted as righteousness, just as Noah's faith was. May we, in our obedience, leave a legacy of righteousness for future generations. In Jesus name we pray, Amen!

The key points of this message entitled "Unsinkable Faith" are as follows:

1. **Introduction:** The message begins by posing questions about having faith in challenging situations and being called by God to fulfill a significant task.
2. **Noah's Story:** It delves into the story of Noah and the Flood from the book of Genesis, highlighting Noah's righteousness and obedience to God's commands in a wicked and corrupt world.
3. **Obedience Amid Ridicule:** Noah is depicted as a man who obeyed God's instructions to build an ark, even though the idea of a catastrophic flood was ridiculed by others. His faith in God's voice guided his actions.
4. **Biblical Reference:** The message quotes Hebrews 11:7, which speaks of Noah's faith and obedience in preparing the ark, and how his faith condemned the world's unbelief.
5. **Noah's Faith in Action:** It discusses how Noah followed God's instructions faithfully, even when there were no clear signs of an impending flood. The analogy of preparing for a snowstorm in the middle of summer illustrates his unwavering trust in God's word.
6. **Facing Ridicule:** Noah and his sons endured ridicule and mockery from those who passed by as they worked on the ark. The devotional relates this to the rejection and threats faced by Jesus and His followers.
7. **Waiting for Light:** The message touches on the symbolism of light in Noah's story, indicating God's incorporation of light into Noah's future. It draws parallels between waiting for the light to reflect off a mountain peak and waiting for Christ's return.
8. **The Legacy of Righteousness:** Despite Noah's obedience, the devotional emphasizes that he was ultimately redeemed by

God's favor, not his own efforts. His faithfulness left a legacy of righteousness.

9. **Application to Today:** The message encourages readers to lead their families with unwavering faith, just as Noah did, by establishing God as the head of their lives and households.

10. **Prayer:** The message concludes with a prayer, thanking God for the message and asking for guidance, direction, and unsinkable faith in the face of challenges.

Overall, this message highlights the importance of unwavering faith and obedience to God's calling, even in the face of ridicule and when circumstances seem illogical. It draws inspiration from Noah's story to encourage readers to trust God's voice and direction in their own lives.

Waiting On God

Moses's job throughout Deuteronomy was to lead Israel to the promised land from Egypt. Moses starts to grow old; the scripture says he reaches 120 years old, and he tells Israel he can no longer act as their leader.

Now, Israel isn't familiar with Joshua just because they were so used to Moses's way of doing things, but the Lord ordains Joshua to take the place of Moses.

Chapter 31, verse 6, reads, "Be strong and courageous, don't be terrified or afraid of them. For the Lord your God is the one who will go with you; he will not leave you nor forsake you or abandon you."

This text really spoke to me, especially in this season of my life, because I feel that it can impact you in every aspect, especially when you feel like you are stuck in a stage where you're supposed to be moving.

This message is entitled "Waiting on God."

You will go through unexpected trials and tribulations in your life that will cause you to get stuck in a stage, and you see, anytime you get stuck in a stage or stay in a place where you think you're intended to move, it will cause you to believe that it is an indication to a conclusion coming in your life, and frankly, this position of being stuck in a stage can happen to anyone.

Deuteronomy 31:6 states that "He will not leave you nor forsake you," and you see, you must be careful when focusing on yourself rather than focusing on God because it's easy to think that God is done with us when we get caught up in ourselves.

There will be times when you want something to happen, and it doesn't, and there will be times in your life when your reality won't meet your expectations, but don't allow these brief stages to allow you to come to the conclusion that God is finished with you just because your plans didn't work out in your time. In other words, be cautious not to place a period where God is only trying to place a comma.

I know that God has great plans for my life, but I also must come to the realization that it's His timing and not mine. It is imperative that you know that everything has a timetable on it. Just like there's the right thing, there's also the right time.

Believe it or not, there's a time for everything under Heaven. The right thing at the wrong time goes negative, so it is crucial that when you are in situations like this, you discipline yourself and train your mind to wait on God.

That's my prayer for you. That you develop that patience because maybe there's a reason why God has you there. It could be to plant a seed, to bless somebody else, to learn something, to grow, to mature, or to nurture something in that season. Just don't place a period where God is only placing a comma.

Prayer:

Heavenly Father,

As we come before You in prayer, we reflect on the message of "Waiting on God." In times when unexpected trials and tribulations make us feel stuck in a particular stage of life, help us to remember the words from Deuteronomy 31:6.

You, Lord, are the one who goes with us. You will not leave us, forsake us, or abandon us. In moments when we are tempted to believe that being stuck is an indication of a conclusion, remind us that Your plans for us are greater than our own. Help us not to focus solely on ourselves but to trust in Your divine timing.

May we not be discouraged when our expectations don't align with our reality. Instead, grant us the wisdom to recognize that there's a purpose in every season. Let us not hastily place a period where You are intending a comma.

Give us the patience to wait on You, understanding that there's a reason for every delay. Whether it's to plant a seed, bless someone else, learn, grow, mature, or nurture something in that season, help us to discern Your purpose in our waiting.

We pray for discipline of mind and spirit, that we may train ourselves to wait on You with hopeful anticipation. Strengthen our faith, O Lord, and help us to embrace the truth that Your timing is perfect. In Jesus name we pray, Amen!

The key points of this message entitled "Waiting On God" are as follows:

1. **Introduction to the Bible Passage:** The author introduces the context of Deuteronomy 31, where Joshua is taking over the leadership from Moses. Moses, due to his old age, cannot continue as their leader, and Joshua is appointed by the Lord.
2. **Scriptural Encouragement:** The author highlights Deuteronomy 31:6, which encourages believers to be strong and courageous, reminding them that God will go with them and will not abandon them.
3. **Stuck in a Stage:** The message addresses the idea that unexpected trials and circumstances in life can make people feel stuck in a particular stage or situation. The feeling of being stuck can lead to the belief that it signifies the end of a particular chapter in one's life.
4. **Focusing on God:** It emphasizes the importance of not solely focusing on oneself during difficult times but remembering that God is always with us and hasn't abandoned us.
5. **God's Timing:** The message encourages patience and highlights that God has a timetable for everything. It stresses that the

right thing at the wrong time can have negative consequences, so waiting on God's timing is crucial.

6. **Purpose in Waiting**: The author suggests that there may be a reason for the season of waiting, such as planting seeds, blessing others, personal growth, or learning important lessons.

7. **Not Putting a Period but a Comma**: The central message is not to prematurely conclude that God is finished with you just because things haven't gone as expected. Instead, it's important to recognize that God might be putting a comma, indicating that there's more to come.

8. **Closing Prayer**: The message concludes with a prayer for those who may be feeling stuck in a stage of life, asking God to grant them patience and faith to trust His timing and purpose.

Overall, this message encourages readers to trust in God's plan and timing, even when facing unexpected trials and periods of waiting in life. It emphasizes the importance of focusing on God's presence and purpose during these times.

Who Are You

_____

God told Abraham, "I will make your name great!" We live in a generation now where people don't really know their purpose. They are just out here living. It makes me wonder if anyone ever has that one question, "Why am I here?" The reason why no one questions if they have purpose anymore is because sometimes we can confuse who we are with what we do.

We think that as long as we wear designer bags, drive foreign cars, live in a brand name housing market, or make over 6 figures a year, that is a representation of who we are. In retrospect, that's not your purpose; that's more so your image. Don't get me wrong, all those things are great, but what good is it to be living like you're full, but in reality, you're empty on the inside.

Join me as I journey through the scriptures and encounter stories of individuals who discovered their true identities in the Lord.

This message is entitled "Who Are You?"

In the book of Genesis, we read that God created mankind in His own image, both male and female. This indicates that we are eternal reflections of God. We are fearfully and wonderfully made, possessing unique gifts and capacities that define who we are.

In the book of Psalms, King David reminds us that we are not accidents or random beings. Psalm 139 reads, "For you created my inmost being; you knit me together in my mother's womb. I praise you because I am fearfully and wonderfully made." This verse assures us that the Lord, in his infinite wisdom, designed each of us with a purpose and plan.

Moses, for example, initially struggled with self-doubt and insecurity. But when he encountered God at the burning bush, he learned that he was chosen to lead the Israelites out of bondage. It was through this encounter that Moses discovered his true identity as a deliverer and leader.

The Apostle Paul experienced a transformation in his understanding of self. Once a persecutor of Christians, he encountered Jesus on the road to Damascus and became a passionate follower of Christ. In his letters, Paul often referred to himself as a "Servant of Christ" and a "prisoner of the Lord," embracing his identity as a chosen instrument for spreading the Gospel.

John the Baptist recognized his identity in relation to Christ, understanding that he was called to prepare the way for the Messiah. He humbly acknowledged that he must decrease while Jesus increased, pointing others to the true identity and purpose of Christ.

Mary Magdalene, a woman who was delivered from demons by Jesus, understood her identity in Christ. She became a devoted follower and witnessed the crucifixion, burial, and resurrection of Jesus. Jesus also entrusted her with the important task of announcing His resurrection to the disciples.

Believe it or not, our time here on Earth is simply a mission trip. Earth isn't our place of residence or our final destination; it is just a part of our journey. Sometimes we can get so stuck on our image to the world that we truly forget that it's not necessarily our purpose we are chasing; it is God's purpose for our lives that we should be in pursuit of.

So, how do we come to know who we truly are? How do we know why we are here on Earth? How did the individuals we named earlier make that shift to fully understand the complexity of why they exist? It all starts by seeking God's wisdom and guidance. Friends, the Bible provides us with a foundation for understanding our identity as children of God. Through prayer, reflection, and studying the Word, we can discern the unique purpose and calling that God has placed upon our lives.

Additionally, we must remember that our identity is not solely based on our own achievements or external validation. Our worth and value come from God's love for us. The apostle John reminds us of this truth in 1 John 3:1 when he writes, "See what great love the Father has lavished on us, that we should be called children of God!"

I for one can personally tell you that I've tried it all. I know what it's like to have the money. I know what it's like to be the driver of a foreign vehicle with the sunroof back blasting loud music. I understand the thrill and temporary pleasure of wearing thousands of dollars' worth of jewelry around your neck. I've witnessed the short-term benefit of being placed on a pedestal and being praised by peers for what the world calls "Success." I know what being the best at something feels like, but all those false narratives that achievements, fame, and money define who you are lead you down a road to self-destruction.

Friends, understanding our identity in Christ is transformative. It liberates us from the shackles of insecurity, comparison, and worldly labels. When we grasp the depth of our identity as image-bearers of God, redeemed and beloved children, co-heirs with Christ, and ambassadors of His kingdom, then and only then can we live with confidence, joy, and purpose.

Remember that knowing who we are is a lifelong journey! From now on, let us turn to the divine guidebook to discover the depths of who we are and the real reason why we are here. May you walk in the assurance of your true identity and live out your calling accordingly.

Jonathyn J. Williams

Prayer:

Heavenly Father,

We come before You with hearts open to the message of "Who Are You?" as we explore the scriptures to understand our true identities in You.

Lord, in the book of Genesis, we are reminded that we are fearfully and wonderfully made, created in Your own image. As we journey through the stories of Moses, Paul, John the Baptist, and Mary Magdalene, we see individuals who discovered their true identities in You.

Psalm 139 reassures us that each of us is intricately designed with a purpose and plan by Your infinite wisdom. Moses, despite his initial struggles, discovered his identity as a deliverer and leader through an encounter with You. Paul transformed from a persecutor to a passionate follower of Christ, embracing his identity as a servant and prisoner of the Lord.

John the Baptist recognized his role in preparing the way for the Messiah, humbly understanding that he must decrease while Jesus increases. Mary Magdalene, delivered from demons by Jesus, became a devoted follower who witnessed His crucifixion, burial, and resurrection.

Lord, we acknowledge that our time on Earth is a mission trip, and sometimes we get stuck chasing an image rather than Your purpose for our lives. Guide us in seeking Your wisdom and guidance through prayer, reflection, and studying Your Word. In Jesus name we pray, Amen!

The key points of this message entitled "Who Are You," are as follows:

1. **Purpose and Identity:** The message begins by addressing the contemporary struggle of people not knowing their purpose and the tendency to confuse one's identity with external factors.

154

2. **Materialism vs. True Purpose:** The emphasis is on the misconception that material possessions, wealth, and societal success represent one's true identity, contrasting this with the idea that these are merely aspects of one's image.

3. **Scriptural Foundation:** The message guides the audience through biblical stories, starting with Genesis, to establish a foundation that humans are created in God's image, fearfully and wonderfully made.

4. **Biblical Examples of Identity Discovery:** Moses, Paul, John the Baptist, and Mary Magdalene are presented as examples of individuals who discovered their true identities through encounters with God.

5. **Earth as a Mission Trip:** The perspective is introduced that our time on Earth is a mission trip, not a permanent residence, and a reminder to focus on God's purpose rather than societal images.

6. **Seeking God's Wisdom:** The message encourages seeking God's wisdom and guidance through prayer, reflection, and studying the Bible as a means of understanding one's unique purpose.

7. **Value Beyond Achievements:** The importance of recognizing that one's identity is not solely based on personal achievements or external validation, but on God's love.

8. **Personal Testimony:** The author shares a personal testimony of experiencing material success and societal acclaim but realizing the emptiness and self-destruction that can result from false narratives.

9. **Transformation in Christ:** Understanding one's identity in Christ is portrayed as transformative, liberating individuals from insecurity, comparison, and worldly labels.

10. **Confidence and Purpose in Identity:** The message concludes by highlighting the confidence, joy, and purpose that come from grasping the depth of one's identity as an image-bearer of God and a co-heir with Christ.

11. **Lifelong Journey of Knowing:** A reminder that understanding one's identity is a lifelong journey, and a call to turn to the Bible as a divine guidebook for self-discovery.

12. **Closing Prayer:** The prayer acknowledges key points from the devotional, seeking God's guidance in understanding true identity, and references biblical stories.

Overall, the goal of this message is for readers to gain an understanding that one's true identity in Christ is transformative while liberating individuals from insecurities, worldly comparisons, and external labels. It invites readers to embark on a lifelong journey to discover their true selves by turning to the Bible as a divine guidebook and living out their callings with confidence, joy, and purpose.

You Are Called

This message is entitled "You Are Called."

Did you know that just because someone is qualified to do something doesn't mean they are called to do it?

Believe it or not, most of the time when we are working towards something, and we look to our left and our right, we see people who look better than us, who dress better than us, who have a bigger home and drive a nicer car than we do, whose family has it all together, who come from a household of wealth, we fall into the assumption that they are the ones called or chosen for it.

Sometimes you're the youngest in the room, you have the least amount of experience, you have no degrees or doctrines to your name, your resume isn't as long as everyone else's, and you feel that there is no way you're the person for the job when your competition is more equipped than you are.

Maybe you're the least likely child in the family, who doesn't seem to have the potential as your other siblings, and your parents wonder if you'd even make it on your own and lack confidence that you'll be successful and do something with your life.

With this being said, it is easy to become discouraged when you are not equipped or qualified for the assignment at hand.

And I want to jump into 1 Samuel and take a look at David's story, and he's going to demonstrate to us that calling is greater than qualifications.

The Lord sent Samuel to Bethlehem to look for a new king from the sons of Jesse after rejecting Saul as the ruler of Israel. Samuel was given the idea to anoint David as the next king of Israel by the Lord. David's older brothers, Abinadab and Shammah, were presented to Samuel by their father Jesse to see which one of them would be the anointed king. All of David's brothers were up to par and well put together. But the Lord spoke to Samuel and told him that neither Abinadab nor Shammah would be king. When Samuel asked Jesse if he had any more boys left, he remembered David.

David was the youngest of Jesse's sons, a farmer and sheep breeder who spent most of his days outdoors. He was young and very frail and wasn't quite built like his brothers. He didn't fit the outward criteria of what it took to be king. But the Lord spoke to Samuel and said anoint him for he is the one! Samuel did as the Lord instructed, and the spirit of the Lord came powerfully on David from that day forward.

Later in the Bible, we get to the most known story of David, and that's when he defeated the powerful Goliath while using the meager tools of a shepherd and the strength of God. The Philistines fled in terror when their hero was killed. With this triumph, David had given Israel its first victory. David showed his bravery by proving he was deserving of being the next King of Israel.

Friends, when God has called you to do something, you don't have to meet the expectations of the world, you don't have to be highly recommended, you don't have to meet the criteria, you don't have to exceed standards, you don't have to be known, and you don't have to meet the qualifications because YOU ARE CALLED! And scripture tells us that "whom the Lord calls-he qualifies".(Romans 8:30)

So don't worry about what you don't have, or what you're missing, or what you lack. When God calls you, that is enough.

And just like the least likely child David, the spirit of the Lord will overflow in you in such a powerful way that no weapon formed against you shall prosper.

And I challenge you this week to continuously remind yourself that YOU ARE CALLED! You may be thinking that at your job site everyone there is a step ahead of you, but YOU ARE CALLED. You may be thinking at school that classes are getting a little harder and it seems that everyone knows a bit more than you do, but YOU ARE CALLED. You may be thinking that the vision that God placed in your head is too far-fetched and out of your comfort zone, but YOU ARE CALLED. You may be thinking being a mother or a father is tougher than you thought, or maybe marriage is more difficult as the months go by, but YOU ARE CALLED.

And remember just because someone is qualified to do something doesn't mean they are called to do it.

Prayer:

Heavenly Father,

As we come before You, we are reminded of the powerful message that "You Are Called." Lord, in a world where qualifications often take precedence, help us to understand the profound truth that calling is greater than qualifications.

We thank You for the example of David, the youngest and least likely in the eyes of the world, but chosen and anointed by You to be a great leader. Lord, may this message resonate deeply within our hearts, especially in moments when we feel underqualified or unequipped for the tasks at hand.

In times when we are tempted to compare ourselves to others who seem more qualified, remind us that Your calling on our lives is sufficient. We are called not based on worldly standards but by Your divine purpose.

Grant us the courage to embrace our calling, even when we don't meet the expectations of the world. Help us to trust that when You call us, You also qualify us. Strengthen our faith and confidence in Your plans for our lives.

May this message inspire and encourage us throughout the week, reminding us that we are called for a purpose, and in Your strength, we can overcome any challenges that come our way. In Jesus name we pray, Amen!

The key points of this message entitled "You Are Called" are as follows:

1. **Qualification vs. Calling:** The message emphasizes that being qualified for something doesn't necessarily mean you are called to do it. Many times, people feel inadequate because they compare themselves to others who seem better equipped or more qualified.
2. **David's Story:** The message references the biblical story of David to illustrate that calling is more significant than qualifications. Despite being the youngest and physically less impressive than his brothers, David was anointed as the next king of Israel by God's choice.
3. **God's Calling:** The central message is that when God calls you to do something, you don't have to meet the world's expectations, criteria, or qualifications. God qualifies those whom He calls, and His calling is enough.
4. **Encouragement:** The message encourages readers to remind themselves that they are called, regardless of the challenges or inadequacies they may perceive. It urges readers to trust in God's calling and not to be discouraged by their circumstances or the qualifications of others.
5. **Prayer:** The message concludes with a prayer, thanking God for the message and asking for blessings on the readers as they go about their day.

Overall, this message demonstrates the importance of recognizing and trusting in God's calling, even when it doesn't align with worldly qualifications or standards. It aims to inspire readers to have faith in their calling and to rely on God's guidance and empowerment to fulfill their purpose.

Thank You Message For Readers

Dear Readers,

I am filled with gratitude as I extend a heartfelt thank you to each and every one of you who has embarked on the journey within the pages of my book. Your decision to explore the world I've created means the world to me.

Writing this book has been a labor of love, and knowing that it found its way into your hands is the most rewarding outcome I could have hoped for.

Books have a unique power to disconnect you with the world for a bit, and I am grateful that you've allowed my words to be a part of your life! Your support is the driving force behind every writer's endeavor, and I feel fortunate to have readers as wonderful as you.

If my book has left you with new perspectives, calmed your mind during a quiet evening, or simply provided a temporary escape, then I consider my mission accomplished. I sincerely hope that you enjoyed the journey as much as I enjoyed crafting it for you.

Please feel free to reach out and share your thoughts—I would love to hear from you. Your feedback is valuable as I continue to grow and evolve as a writer.

Once again, thank you for choosing to spend your time with my words. May the stories you discover in these 30 messages linger in your thoughts long after you've closed the book.

Much love,
Jonathyn J. Williams

www.ingramcontent.com/pod-product-compliance
Lightning Source LLC
Chambersburg PA
CBHW051826040426
42447CB00006B/393